Just Right

Ana Acevedo
Carol Lethaby
Jeremy Harmer

Workbook
with answer key

Marshall Cavendish
Education

Photo acknowledgements

p.5 ©Stock Connection Distribution/Alamy; p.7 tl ©Oxford Picture Library/Alamy, a ©Stock Connection Distribution/Alamy, b ©AlanWylie/Alamy, c ©Leslie Garland Picture Library/Alamy, d ©The Image Bank/Getty Images, e ©Matthias Kulka/Zefa/Corbis, f ©Mark Sykes/Alamy, g ©The Hoberman Collection/Alamy, h ©David Sanger photography/Alamy; p.10 l ©Keren Su/Corbis, r Michael Juno/Alamy; p.15 ©Ken McKay/Rex Features; p.20 ©Liam Bailey/Alamy; p.30 ©Mary Evans Picture Library/Alamy; p.32 ©Photofusion Picture Library/Alamy; p.35 a ©Tim de Waele/Corbis, b ©Marco Cristofori/Iconica/Getty Images, c ©Shout/Alamy, d ©Popperfoto/Alamy, e ©The Image Bank/Getty Images, f ©Taxi/Getty Images, g ©Photonica/Getty Images, h ©Stone/Getty Images, I ©Adrian Sherratt/Alamy, j ©Allsport Concepts/Getty Images; p.38 ©Stone/Getty Images; p.40 a ©Everynight Images/Alamy, b ©Royalty Free/Corbis; p.43 ©Owen Franken/Corbis;   p.56 ©Chuck Savage/Corbis; p.58 ©Stone/Getty Images; p.59 a ©Stone/Getty Images, b ©Image100/Photolibrary.com; p.61 top ©Sipa Press/Rex Features, bottom ©Sophie Bassouls/Corbis; p.71 ©Andre Jenny/Alamy; p.82 a ©Michael S. Yamashita/Corbis, b ©William Whitehurst/Corbis

Marshall Cavendish Education
119 Wardour Street
London W1F 0UW
www.mcelt.com/justright

Designed by Hart McLeod, Cambridge
Editorial development by msfoundry

Printed and bound by Times Offset (M) Sdn. Bhd. Malaysia

Contents

UNIT 1 The world of English

Study grammar: comparative adjectives and adverbs

➡ see 1A in the Mini-grammar

1 Complete the sentences with the comparative form of the adjectives and adverbs in brackets. Add *than* only where necessary.

a Cities are ...~~more interesting~~... (interesting) .... beaches, but you can relax .... (easily) .... at the beach.

b The food in Australia is .... (good) .... here, and you can eat .... (cheaply) .... too!

c Where is the public transport .... (fast) .... , in London or in Dublin? In Dublin, probably, and Dublin is .... (small) .... , so you can walk.

d I find travelling by train .... (comfortable) .... travelling by car and you can also get there .... (quickly) ....

e Plane fares to New Zealand are .... (low) in July .... in December. But it's .... (cold) .... then because it's winter there.

2 Read the information about the package holidays to Barbados, an island in the Caribbean. Use the adjectives in the box to write 8 comparative sentences.

	Package 1	Package 2	Package 3
Dates	20–27 December	10–18 April	5–14 July
Temperature	25C	22C	30C
Duration of flight	9 hours (direct flight)	12 hours (one stop)	16 hours (one stop)
Hotels	Hotel Tropicana	Paradise Resort	Hotel Toucan
Comfort	*****	***	****
Includes	All meals and drinks	Room only	Breakfast and dinner
	2 tours to places of interest Boat tour	All sports equipment and facilities	Organised sports activities
Prices	$1,980 US	$1,860 US	$999 US

hot ◆ cool ◆ expensive ◆ cheap ◆ long ◆ short ◆ interesting ◆ fun ◆ comfortable ◆ attractive ◆ good

1 *Package 1 is more expensive then Package 3.*
2 ....
3 ....
4 ....
5 ....
6 ....
7 ....
8 ....

3 Which package is better for you? Why? Write four sentences explaining your reasons.

Example: *Package 1 is better.*
   1 You can get to Barbados more quickly.
   2 It is more expensive but...

1 ....
2 ....
3 ....
4 ....

4 Complete the dialogue with expressions from the box. Then listen to Track 1.1 and check your answers.

5 Listen to Track 1.2. Read out Sam's words after the beep.

> I'd rather... ◆ Which do you prefer ◆ I prefer ◆ Would you rather

SAM: Which package is better, then?

JACK: Oh, Package 3, definitely. It's cheaper! (a) *Which do you prefer* ?

SAM: Me? I prefer Package 1. It sounds much nicer.

JACK: But it's more expensive and shorter. Anyway, (b) .... summer holidays to winter holidays.

SAM: But the summer is nice here, too. (c) .... go in December, when it's dark and cold here.

JACK: OK, you win. But that's the only holiday we can take in the whole the year then. (d) .... have just one holiday or two? Think about it.

SAM: Oh. Maybe July is not so bad after all...

Study reading and grammar: *–ing* and *–ed* adjectives

➡ see 1B in the Mini-grammar

6 Read the postcards. Match them with the pictures.

a

have a cuppa

b

english weather

Here I am in England, finally! I'm so (a) excited/exciting! Some things are (b) surprised/surprising, some are even (c) shocked/shocking. The weather is particularly (d) interested/interesting. Today it rained all day and it was cold. Now, at 9 p.m., the sun is shining! One thing is sure: things are different but never (e) bored/boring!

Wish you were here!

David

'How about a cuppa?' That's what my friend asks me all the time! She means 'a cup of tea'. Here people drink tea when they are cold, or hot, when they are (f) tired/tiring, or (g) relaxed/relaxing... Tea always makes you feel better! But nobody has the famous four o'clock tea, like it says in our English book. That's very (h) disappointed/disappointing!

Lucy

Study vocabulary: two-word nouns

9 Match the words in the boxes to make two-word nouns. Use the two-word nouns to label the pictures.

cricket	match
letter	station
car	box
phone	park
road	bag
tea	signs
traffic	lights
underground	box

a

b

c

d

g

7 Underline the correct word in the postcards. The first one is done for you.

8 Complete each sentence with the correct *-ing* or *-ed* adjective from the verb in brackets.

a Driving on the left was a bit
  ...frightening.. (frighten) at first.

b I am a bit ....
  (worry) about my English.

c I went to a cricket match.

  It was long and ....

  (bore).

d English food is very good.

  That's .... (surprise),
  isn't it?

e People say English humour is

  very .... (amuse) but I
  don't understand it.

f I am .... (interest) in
  British pop music.

e

f

h

a ....phone box....	d	g ....
b	e	h ....
c	f	

10 Write two-word nouns for the definitions.

  a a shop where you can buy books

  a book shop

  b a sandwich made with chicken

  ....

  c a shop where you can buy music

  ....

  d a cake made with fruit

  ....

  e a biscuit made with chocolate

  ....

11 Word Bank. Practise your new words.

  a Write new words from this unit on small cards.
  b Draw a picture and write a translation on the other side of the card.
  c Put the cards in a box or a bag and mix them up.
  d Take them out one at a time. Be careful to look only at one side. If it is the picture/translation, say the English word. If it is the English word, translate it into your language.
  e Check you were right by turning the card over.

Pronunciation: stress in two-word nouns

12 Read the words to yourself. Underline the stressed word in the two-word nouns.

  a <u>phone</u> box
  b letter box
  c tea cup
  d road signs
  e park bench
  f traffic lights
  g cricket match
  h underground station

13 Listen to Track 1.3 and repeat the words. Were your answers correct?

14 Add the stress to the words in your Word Bank. Do this to difficult words you meet as you go on learning.

How did you do?

15 Can you translate these sentences into your language?

a Planes travel faster than trains.

....

b Canada is bigger than Australia.

....

c Cities are more exciting than beaches.

....

d Is there a phone box near here?

....

e I'd rather stay at home this summer.

....

f Learning about other countries is interesting.

....

g I am interested in other countries.

....

16 Evaluation of Just learning in Unit 1

Answer these questions about the Just learning section in Unit 1 page 6 of the Student's Book.

Listening for general meaning

When would you *listen for general meaning*? Tick the boxes below.

▓ You are listening to the football results on the radio.

▓ You are listening to someone giving you directions in the street.

▓ You are listening to the news on the radio to find out what's happening in the world.

▓ You are listening to a story and want to know what it is about.

When did you last *listen for general meaning* in English? Explain what happened.

....

....

....

....

....

17 Phonetics

Look at the phonemic symbols on page 96. Write these words from Unit 1 in normal spelling.

a /ɒstˈreɪliə/ _Australia_

b /njuː ˈziːlənd/ ....

c /ɡreɪt ˈbrɪtən/ ....

d /ˈaɪrlənd/ ....

e /dʒəˈmeɪkə/ ....

f /ˈskɒtlənd/ ....

g /ðə juːesˈeɪ/ ....

Listen to Track 1.4 to check your answers and then read the words aloud.

UNIT 2 | Don't get stressed out!

Study grammar: countable and uncountable nouns

➡ see 6B in the Mini-grammar

1 Read this leaflet. Write the nouns in green in the correct place in the chart below.

Stressed out? Try Tai Chi

When you have many things to do and no time to do them all, the result is often stress. Stress is a part of modern living. It is bad for your mind and bad for your body. Tai Chi is a good way to reduce stress.

What is Tai Chi?
Tai Chi is an old Chinese form of exercise. The movements increase the energy inside you, or your 'chi'.

How does it work?
The exercises in Tai Chi are very slow and controlled. When you do tai chi, your think only of the movement and your breathing. Energy moves inside you body and you become stronger and calmer – and less stressed.

Who can do Tai Chi?
People of all ages. You don't have to be very strong and you don't need any special equipment. Wear comfortable clothes and comfortable shoes – or you can do it without shoes.

2 Label the nouns underlined in the text below C (countable) or U (uncountable).

The answer to stress? A good, healthy diet!

➡ First, eat less sugar [U] and oil [ ]. So, things like cakes [ ] and cookies [ ] and fried potatoes [ ] are never a good idea.

➡ Cut down on red meat [ ] – have chicken [ ] and fish [ ] instead.

➡ Eat only small quantities of rice [ ] and pasta [ ]. A few boiled potatoes are fine too.

➡ Plan your healthy meals to include yoghurt [ ], vegetables [ ] and plenty of fruit [ ] (but be careful! Fruit juice [ ] has a lot of sugar).

Countable nouns (C)	things
Uncountable nouns (U)	stress
Countable and uncountable	exercise exercises

3 In a, b and c, first decide which nouns are countable and which are uncountable. Then complete the exercises.

a Write *a* or *an* before the nouns, where possible.

a ...*a*... shoe

b .... exercise

c .... chicken

d .... stress

e .... clothes

f .... equipment

g .... orange

h .... furniture

i .... fish

b Write the plural form of the nouns, where possible.

advice ....

cheese ....

paper ....

furniture ....

information ....

homework ....

milk ....

apple ....

rice ....

c Circle the nouns that can be countable and uncountable.

salad   soup   stress   coffee

cake   fruit   chocolate   butter

clothing

Study vocabulary: phrases with uncountable nouns

4 Look at this picture of someone's lunch. Label it with phrases 'a ... of ...'. Choose words from the chart below. You will need to use some of the words twice.

5 ....

7 ....

6 ....

3

2

4 ....

1   *a bowl of soup*

a	bowl cup drop glass jug pinch tablespoon slice plate	of	bread cake coffee cream ice cream orange juice rice salt soup tea water lemon

5 Add more nouns to the right hand column of the chart in Activity 4, such as *salad*, *meat*, etc.
Use your words to make up two other lunch 'menus' and write them in your notebook.

Example: *a bowl of salad, a cup of hot chocolate with a tablespoon of cream,...*

6 Word Bank

  a Make a special Word Bank notebook. Write new phrases from this section. Draw a picture, or write a translation for each word.

  b Revise your words every now and then: look at the words and their meaning and say the phrases aloud.

  c Choose some of the words and phrases in this section. Put them on cards and add them to your bag or box (see Word Bank, Unit 1 of the Workbook).

Study grammar: talking about quantities

➡ see 6C in the Mini-grammar

7 Choose the right words to complete the sentences. Decide first whether the nouns are countable or uncountable.

  a I haven't got ....much.... (much/many) free time during the week but at the weekend I have .... (many/lots of) time to see my friends.

  b I have .... (much/many) friends, but only .... (a few/a little) good friends.

  c We have to go shopping: there isn't .... (many/much) food in the fridge and there is .... (any/no) milk at all.

  d Is there .... (any/some) coffee? Yes, but we haven't got .... (some/any) sugar.

  e In the past, I had .... (a few/not many) problems sleeping. Now I haven't got .... (some/any) and I feel great!

8 Write about yourself. Write four sentences like sentence **a** and four sentences like sentence **b**. Use words and phrases from the boxes.

> lots of ◆ a lot of ◆ a few ◆ a little ◆ some ◆
> not many ◆ not much ◆ no ◆ any

> good friends ◆ time ◆ problems ◆ pop CDs ◆ energy ◆ work ◆
> food in the fridge ◆ old boyfriends/girlfriends ◆ brothers and sisters

  a I've got <u>lots of good friends</u>.

    ....

    ....

    ....

    ....

  b I haven't got <u>many problems</u>.

    ....

    ....

    ....

    ....

Functional language: asking for and giving advice

9 Leyla is asking Rob for advice. Rob is trying to help. Choose from the expressions in the chart and complete the dialogue.

Asking for advice	Giving advice
Can you give me some advice?	Try ...
Got any (ideas)?	How about ...?
What can I do ...?	You can do ...
	You could ...

ROB: Hi Leyla! You don't look too happy. Problems?

LEYLA: I have exams next week and I don't know anything! (a) _What can I do_ to pass?

ROB: Hey, relax! (b) .... studying your notes.

LEYLA: Yeah, I looked at them, but it doesn't help.

ROB: Well, of course, just <u>looking</u> doesn't help. You (c) .... some of the practice questions, too.

LEYLA: Hmm, yes. But what about maths? I don't understand anything! (d) .... ideas?

ROB: Well, you (e) .... do some of the exercises in the book. Don't worry! That's my advice!

LEYLA: You're right. Let's forget about exams. Do you want to listen to my new JLo record?

Listen to Track 2.1 to check your answers.

10 You are Rob. Listen to Track 2.2 and read out Rob's words after the beep.

Pronunciation: word stress

11 Listen to Track 2.3. Listen first to the examples (a and b) and look at their stress shapes.

a problem ⬜☐

b result ☐⬜

Now listen to Track 2.4 and draw the shapes of the words you hear.

c coffee ....

d chocolate ....

e water ....

f inside ....

g salad ....

h without ....

i practise ....

12 Listen to Track 2.4 again. Check you got the shapes right. Repeat the words.

How did you do?

13 Find the mistake and write the correct version.

wrong	right
a I bought a new baseball equipment.	I bought new baseball equipment.
b Don't put no sugar in your tea.	
c Can you lend me some moneys?	
d Did you buy a sugar?	
e Have a few butter on your bread.	
f He has many money!	
g I want only a little vegetables.	
h Can you give me an advice?	
i You could to try some exercise.	
j What can I do for to cook a nice meal?	

14 Evaluation of Just learning in Unit 2

Answer these questions about the Just learning section in Unit 2 page 15 of the Student's Book.

> Predicting the content of a text
>
> Which of these things did you do the last time you *predicted the content of a text*?
> Tick the boxes below.
>
> ▓ I looked at the pictures.
>
> ▓ I tried to think where the text came from.
>
> ▓ I thought about things I already knew about the topic.
>
> ▓ Other (write what).
>
> ....
>
> ....
>
> ....
>
> ....
>
> ....

15 Phonetics

Look at the phonemic symbols on page 96. Write these words from Unit 2 in normal spelling.

a /'tʃɒklət/   chocolate ....

b /'kɒfiː/   ....

c /mʌtʃ/   ....

d /fjuː/   ....

e /əd'vaɪs/   ....

f /'meni/   ....

◁) Listen to Track 2.5 to check your answers and then read the words aloud.

UNIT 3 TV and the media

Study Grammar: *the present simple*

⇒ see 10A in the Mini-grammar

1 Read the article. Fill in the blanks with the correct form of the present simple of the verbs in brackets.

Presenting *Breakfast*: a dream job?

Breakfast is a programme on British television. The presenters
(a) ...interview... (interview) people and **(b)** .... (read)
the news. Millions of viewers **(c)** .... (watch) it every day.
Breakfast is on air live from 6 to 9.15 every morning. This
(d) .... (mean) a very early start for the presenters,
Dermot Murnaghan and Natasha Kaplinski. Natasha
(e) .... (get up) at 3.15. Dermot **(f)** .... (not get
up) so early but they both **(g)** .... (arrive) at the studios
at 4.30.
First they **(h)** .... (meet) with the producer of the
programme. Natasha and Dermot usually **(i)** ....
(interview) about 12 people everyday so they **(j)** ....
(prepare) carefully – and fast! Then, they have to make sure they
look good.
So **(k)** .... they .... (enjoy) their job? 'It's
fantastic,' says Natasha. 'But the working hours are terrible'.
Natasha **(l)** .... (go) to bed at 8 o'clock and she
(m) .... (try) to go to sleep by 9. When **(n)** ....
she .... (see) her friends? At lunchtime. She
(o) .... (not have) any other time!

So, do you think presenting *Breakfast* is a dream job?

2 Write examples from the text for each use of the present simple, a, b and c.

a We use the present simple to talk about repeated actions and habits.

   Natasha gets up at 3.15.

   ....

   ....

   ....

   ....

b We use the present simple to talk about general facts which are true and will be for some time.

   ....

   ....

   ....

   ....

   ....

c We use the present simple to describe what happens in a film, book, television or radio programme.

   ....

   ....

   ....

   ....

   ....

3 Interview Natasha. Write questions for the answers. Read the article again if you need to.

a YOU: What *is your job/do you do for a living* ?
NATASHA: I am a TV presenter. I present *Breakfast* with Dermot.

b YOU: What time .... ?
NATASHA: It starts at 6 and finishes at 9.15.

c YOU: What time .... ?
NATASHA: Very early. At 3.15!

d YOU: .... get up at 3.15 too?
NATASHA: No. He gets up a little later but we start work at the same time.

e YOU: When .... ?
NATASHA: My friends? I see them at lunchtime – It's the only time I have!

f YOU: .... your job?
NATASHA: I love my job! But I don't really like the working hours.

4 Put the words in the correct order to write three more questions for Natasha. Don't forget the capital letter at the beginning of each question.

a do / for / time / you / have / breakfast / ? /
Do you have time for breakfast?

b days / do / work / you / how many / week / a / ? /
....

c your family / what / think / about / does/ working hours / your / ? /
....
....

d you / lots of / buy / new clothes / do / for work / ? /
....

Study vocabulary: reading, watching, listening

5 Read the situations. Write sentences to tell the people what to do, as in the example. Use these verbs and phrases.

read	a comic	an article
watch	a magazine	a film
listen to	a newspaper	the radio
	a programme	television
	the news	the weather forecast

a JAKE: I want to know what is new in the world. What can I do?
YOU: *Well, you could read the newspaper, or listen to the news* .

b CAROLINE: What can I do to find out about the new fashions?
YOU: ....

c Your eight-year-old neighbour: I'm bored! Got any ideas?
YOU: ....

d CINDY: This flight is so long!
YOU: ....

e ANYA: Shall I take an umbrella? Is it going to rain?
YOU: ....

f JOE: I have a cold. I have to stay in bed all day! What can I do?
YOU: ....

g PAM: I've finished my book and I'm still waiting to see the dentist! What can I do now?
YOU: ....

6 Word Bank

Using new words in sentences helps you to remember them better. Write sentences with these words in your Word Bank notebook.

documentary ◆ soap opera ◆ sitcom ◆ cartoon ◆ game show ◆ talk show ◆ reality show

Example: *My favourite sitcom is Friends.*

➡ see 10A in the Mini-grammar

7 Nancy and Norah are identical twins, but they are very different. Unscramble the lines and complete the sentences with Norah and/or Nancy. Look at 10A in the Mini-grammar for help.

a ..Nancy.. likes trees and flowers.

b .... admires Bono (and her sister, secretly).

c .... reads romantic novels. .... reads her sister's diary (secretly!)

d .... watches soap operas and .... watches documentaries.

e .... admires Bono.

f .... loves Barry. .... does too.

g Does Barry love .... ? No. He only loves his rock band.

8 Complete the questions about Nancy and Norah. Use the verbs in brackets.

a What _does Nancy like_ (like)? Trees and flowers.

b Who _likes_ (like) trees and flowers? Nancy does.

c Who .... (love) Barry? Both girls do.

d What .... (love)? His rock band.

e What programmes .... (watch)? Soap operas.

f Who .... (admire) Bono? Both girls do.

g Who .... (admire)? Bono and her sister.

h Who .... (admire) Nancy? Norah does.

i What .... (read)? Her sister's diary (secretly!).

j Who .... (watch) television? Both girls do.

9 Complete and answer the questions about you. Use the verbs in brackets.

a Who ..._buys_.. (buy) you presents?

My grandmother does ....

b What .... _you_ .... (do) in the evenings?

....

c What .... (make) you really happy?

....

Study functions: discussing opinions

10 Match the beginnings of the sentences in column 1 with the correct groups of endings in column 2.

column 1 (beginnings)	column 2 (endings)

1 What do you think
2 Do you really
3 I (don't) agree
4 I hate
5 I think
	a documentaries about animals.
	   watching the news.
	   rap.
	b of documentaries?
	   of street surveys?
	   of Peter?
	c so, too.
	   you're right.
	   they're interesting.
	d with you.
	   that documentaries are boring.
	   with your ideas.
	e think so?
	   think soaps are stupid?
	   like watching TV?

11 Complete the dialogue with sentences from Exercise 10. Then listen to Track 3.1 and check your answers.

LOUISE: What (a) _do you think of_ documentaries?

DAMIAN: I think they're boring.

LOUISE: Do you really (b) .... ?

DAMIAN: Yes, don't you?

LOUISE: No. (c) .... Well, sometimes.

DAMIAN: (d) .... Only sometimes. I hate

(e) .... , for example.

LOUISE: Oops! I bought you a DVD about birds for your birthday.
DAMIAN: You're joking!
LOUISE: No. I really did.
DAMIAN: Oh, well, birds are fine. Birds are good. Actually, I love birds!

12 Listen to Track 3.2. You are Louise. Read out her lines when you hear the 'beep'. Louise begins the dialogue, so be ready to speak first.

Pronunciation: /ʃ/ and /ʒ/

13 The words in italics in the dialogues below have the sounds /ʃ/ or /ʒ/ in them. Write the words in italics under the correct sound.

/ʃ/
sugar
....
....
....
....

/ʒ/
....
....
....
....

a A: How do you like your tea?
   B: With *sugar*, *usually*.
b A: Come on then. What's the solution?
   B: There is no *solution*. That's my *conclusion*.
c A: What are you doing?
   B: Watching a *fashion* show on *television*.
d A: So, what do you think?
   B: We can make a *decision* after our *discussion*.

14 Listen to Track 3.3. Check your answers. Then listen again and repeat the words.

15 Listen to Track 3.4. Read the answers (part B) in the dialogues above in Exercise 13 when it's your turn.

How did you do?

16 Can you translate these sentences into your language?

a   In this programme the presenters interview people.

....

b   Dermot gets up early.

....

c   Millions of viewers watch the programme.

....

d   Natasha doesn't go out in the evening.

....

e   Who wants to work in television?

....

f   Where does he want to work?

....

g   What makes you laugh?

....

h   You're joking!

....

i   Sorry. I don't agree with you.

....

17 Evaluation of Just learning in Unit 3

Answer these questions about the Just learning section in Unit 3 page 22 of the Student's Book.

Skimming

When is *skimming* useful? Tick the boxes below.

▉ You want to know what a text is about quickly.

▉ You want to find out if a text has the information you want.

▉ You want to decide if you want to read a magazine article in detail.

▉ You want to see if a text is useful for a project.

When was the last time you skimmed a text? Why did you skim it?

....

....

....

....

....

18 Phonetics

Look at the phonemic symbols on page 96. Write these words from Unit 3 in normal spelling.

a   /wɒtʃ/   ....*watch*........

b   /wɒt/   ....

c   /'reɪdɪəʊ/   ....

d   /'juːʒuəl/   ....

e   /ə'griː/   ....

f   /'miːdɪə/   ....

Listen to Track 3.5 to check your answers and then read the words aloud.

UNIT 4 Making a living

Study grammar: the present continuous and the present simple

➧ see 10A and 10B in the Mini-grammar

1 Read these four sentences.

Which ones are about regular or habitual actions? Mark them R/H.

Which are about temporary actions or actions happening at the moment of speaking? Mark them T.

a Tony lives with his parents.　[R/H]
b Sonya is living in Liverpool.　[　]
c What are you doing there?　[　]
d What do you do there?　[　]

2 Complete the blanks with the correct form of the present simple or present continuous of the verbs in brackets.

When he was young, Marco's parents had a restaurant. He loved helping in the kitchen and by the age of 12 he was a pretty good cook. Now, Marco (a) _wants_ (want) to be a chef – a famous chef. But he (b) _____ (know) it is a hard job.
At the moment, Marco (c) _____ (train) to be a chef in college. To get experience (and a little money!) he (d) _____ (work) in a restaurant at night. He (e) _____ (not do) interesting jobs at the moment: he (f) _____ (wash) dishes and (g) _____ (prepare) things for the chef every day. How (h) _____ he _____ (feel) about it? 'It's only temporary,' he says. 'And it's all part of the training.'
'The best cook I know is my mother', Marco says. 'So I (i) _____ (write) down all her secrets little by little. Maybe one day I'll write a book. But at the moment I (j) _____ just _____ (work) hard and (k) _____ (learn) as much as I can.'

3 You interviewed Marco. Write questions for Marco's answers. Use the present simple or the present continuous.

a YOU: _What do you know about a chef's job_ ?

MARCO: Well, I know it's hard!

b YOU: _____
_____ ?

MARCO: A famous chef.

c YOU: _____
_____ in college?

MARCO: I'm training to be a chef.

d YOU: _____
_____ at the moment?

MARCO: In a restaurant.

e YOU: _____
_____ ?

MARCO: I wash dishes and help the chef.

f YOU: _____
_____ ?

MARCO: Because she is the best cook I know!

g YOU: _____
_____ ?

MARCO: No, I'm not. But, who knows? Maybe one day I will write one.

Study vocabulary: jobs and work

4 Complete the sentences with *work* or *job*.

a What's your father's ......job...... ?

b Does he usually have a lot of .... ?

c I like doing projects, but they are hard ....

d Would you like to get a .... for the holidays?

e Charlie graduated from university last month. He needs to get a .... but he doesn't know what kind of .... he wants to do.

5 Complete the sentences with one of the prepositions below. Then unscramble the words in bold to find out the person's occupation.

as ◆ for ◆ in ◆ on ◆ out ◆ with

a Peter works .....in.... a club. His job is to throw out people who behave badly. Peter works as a **cernubo** .....bouncer..... .

b Joni works .... a school. Her job is to teach English. She works .... children. At the moment she is working .... her students' marks. Joni works .... a **achteer** ....

c Lola works .... a radio station. Her job is to play music. At the moment she is working .... a project for a special show: she's working .... the money she needs. She works .... a **sidc yckoje** ....

d Ollie works .... a large company. He works .... animals. His job is to catch rats and other pests. Ollie works .... a **tsep nerctrollo** ....

e Rose works .... a famous band. She works .... sound equipment, like microphones. Her job is to check the equipment before a concert. She is working .... the preparations for a big concert. Rose works .... a **riedoa** ....

6 Word Bank.

Make a diagram like this in your Word Bank notebook. Write the words in Exercise 5 in the right place. Can you add more words for each preposition?

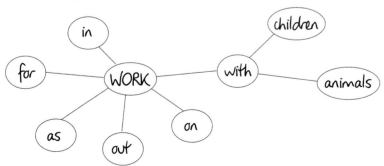

Study pronunciation: intonation of *yes/no* questions

7 Listen to Track 4.1. Does the speaker's voice go up or down?

Listen again and repeat the questions.

a Are you looking for a job? ↑ ....

b Are you interested in people? ....

c Are you good with animals? ....

d Can you work in a team? ....

e Do you like working with animals? ....

8 Listen to the radio advertisement in Track 4.2. Does the speaker say the questions with the same intonation as in Exercise 7? Underline the question where the intonation is different.

Then practise reading the advert aloud.

Are you looking for a job?

How would you like to help animals?

Can you work in a team?

Yes?

We've got the perfect job for you!

Call the Animal Hospital **NOW!**

No experience required!

Study grammar: present continuous with future meaning

➠ see 4B in the Mini-grammar

9 Read these sentences. Do they have future or present meanings?
Write F (future) or P (present) in the brackets.

a Are you still looking for a job? [P]
b Julie's taking a photography course all week. [ ]
c They're showing the same film at the cinema again next week. [ ]
d What are you doing under the table? [ ]
e Are you enjoying your work? [ ]
f I can't go out tonight. I'm baby sitting my baby sister. [ ]
g Everybody's getting a job this summer. [ ]

10 Write each sentence twice, once with present meaning and once with future meaning. Use time expressions from the box.

at the moment ◆ (later) tonight ◆ (right) now ◆ from Monday ◆ next week ◆ at present ◆ this morning ◆ this week

a We're watching a DVD.

We're watching a DVD now. .... (present)

We're watching a DVD tonight. .... (future)

b I'm taking an English lesson.

....

....

c We are doing some grammar exercises.

....

....

d He's working on a new project.

....

....

e Are you working?

.... ?

.... ?

11 Write three fun things you are doing this week and three things you don't really want to do.

Examples: I'm having a party on Saturday.
I'm going to the dentist on Tuesday.

12 Complete the dialogue with the verbs and phrases in the box.
Then listen to Track 4.3 and check your answers.

> love ◆ (don't) like ◆ fancy ◆ keen on ◆ can't stand ◆ don't mind ◆ hate

MAX: I am thinking of teaching after college. But I'm not sure.

MOLLY: Teaching? You? But you (a) *don't like* children.

MAX: I am not very (b) .... them. But I don't (c) ....

them. Actually, I (d) .... really .... children – for a
short time!

MOLLY: I (e) .... little children but I (f) .... big groups.

I (g) .... a job teaching small groups.

MAX: Oh no, that's not for me. I want to get a temporary job to see
if I like it.

MOLLY: That's a good idea.

13 Read these small ads. Which job is better for Molly, which is better
for Max? Complete the sentences using their likes and dislikes.

a I think the job at The Montessori Infant School of Purley is better for

..... *Molly* ..... . She ..... *loves...* ..... .

....

....

b The job at The School on the Hill is better for .... He/she

....

....

c A career in teaching is not really good for .... because

....

14 Write answers for the questions. Then listen to Track 4.4 and
answer when it is your turn.

Example: INTERVIEWER: *How do you feel about children?*

YOU: *I'm really keen on working with children.*

1 INTERVIEWER: How do you feel about children?

YOU: ....

2 INTERVIEWER: Right. Now tell me two things you like about teaching.

YOU: ....

3 INTERVIEWER: And two things you definitely don't like?

YOU: ....

4 INTERVIEWER: So, do you think teaching is right for you?

YOU: ....

> **Are you looking for
> a career in teaching?**
>
> The Montessori School
> of Purley offers:
>
> Free training
>
> Teaching small groups of
> 4–6-year-olds
>
> Good career prospects
>
> Graduates only

> **Attention graduates!!**
>
> The School on the Hill is
> looking for part-time
> classroom assistants on our
> summer programme.
>
> 8 hours per week
>
> Friendly atmosphere
>
> Good pay

How did you do?

15 Find the mistake and write the correct version.

wrong	right
a She reads a good book now.	She is reading a good book now.
b I training to be a chef.	
c What do you do under the bed?	
d Learning English is hard job.	
e He has two works, one in the mornings and one in the evenings.	
f Tomorrow I do my project.	
g What happened? Why do you cry?	

16 Evaluation of Just learning in Unit 4

Answer these questions about the Just learning section in Unit 4 page 30 of The Student's Book.

Guessing word meaning in a reading text

When would you try to *guess the meaning* of new words? Tick the boxes below.

- ☐ You are looking for information on an English web site.

- ☐ You are reading an article quickly to find out the general idea.

- ☐ You are reading the instructions for electronic equipment.

- ☐ You are reading an advertisement for a job.

Describe what happened the last time you tried to *guess the meaning* of a word. What word was it? Did you guess correctly?

....

....

....

....

....

17 Phonetics

Look at the phonemic symbols on page 96. Write these words from Unit 4 in normal spelling.

a /dʒɒb/ .... job ....

b /ˈtʃekɪŋ/ ....

c /wɜːk/ ....

d /pleɪɪŋ/ ....

e /dʌz/ ....

f /lʌv/ ....

Listen to Track 4.5 to check your answers and then read the words aloud.

UNIT 5 | On the move

Study grammar: prepositions of place

➠ see 9A in the Mini-grammar

1 Where is the ball? Use one of these prepositions to say where the ball is in relation to the table(s).

above ◆ behind ◆ between ◆ on top of ◆ next to ◆ under

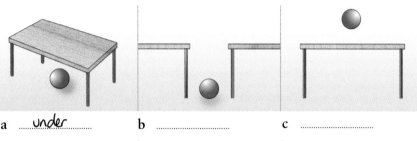

a _under_   b _____   c _____

d _____   e _____   f _____

2 Now complete these sentences about this picture.

a The computer is inside _the wardrobe_ .

b _____ is opposite the door.

c The cap is outside _____ .

d There is _____ inside a box.

e Below _____ there is a desk.

f The chair is in front of _____ .

3 Write as many sentences about this picture as you can.

_____
_____
_____
_____
_____
_____
_____
_____
_____
_____
_____
_____
_____
_____
_____
_____

4 Match the word to the meaning.

> bay • escalator • gate • lift • airport • barrier •
> board • platform • ticket • terminal

a a moving staircase *escalator*

b a place where you can get onto the train

....

c a piece of paper you need to travel on a train, plane or bus ....

d the place where you can take a plane

....

e a small room that carries people up and down

....

f the verb that means to 'get onto' a plane, train or bus ....

g the place where people wait before they get on the plane ....

h a thing that stops movement ....

i a place where you can take a ferry ....

j a place where you can get on a bus ....

5 Complete this paragraph with the correct verb.

> arrive • board • leave • check in •
> go • leave • take • go

Taking the plane

If you want to **(a)** *take* a plane to travel, you will need to **(b)** .... to an airport. There you need to **(c)** .... at least one hour before your flight. You have to **(d)** .... by showing your ticket at a desk, and you also **(e)** .... your luggage here. You then need to **(f)** .... to your departure gate and wait. About thirty minutes before you are going to **(g)** ...., you can **(h)** .... the plane.

6 Complete this description with the correct word.

Lindy arrived at the *airport* and went immediately to the c_ _ _ _ -i_ d_ _ _ and she showed her t_ _ _ _ _ . She was flying to Brazil so she went up the e_ _ _ _ _ _ _ _ to the international t_ _ _ _ _ _ _ . It took her ten minutes to walk to her g_ _ _ . She b_ _ _ _ _ _ the plane. At the end of the flight, when she a_ _ _ _ _ _ in Brazil, she had to go through p_ _ _ _ _ _ _ c_ _ _ _ _ _ . Then she picked up her L_ _ _ _ _ _ and t_ _ _ a t_ _ _ to her hotel.

7 Word Bank

Make a table like this in your Word Bank notebook. Put all the travel words you can find in this unit into the appropriate column. Some can go in more than one column. Add any other words you know that are not in the unit.

plane	train	bus
ticket	ticket	ticket
airport	platform	

Study functions: arranging to meet

8 Put these sentences in the right order to make a dialogue.

  a JACKIE: Where's the best place to meet?
  b SANDY: See you there.
  c JACKIE: Hmm. How about 7.30?
  d JACKIE: Why don't we meet at Café Commons?
  e JACKIE: OK. 7.30 it is, then.
  f SANDY: OK. What time?
  g SANDY: That sounds great.
  h SANDY: Where do you suggest?

  _a_ ....

Now listen to Track 5.1 to check your answers.

9 Complete this dialogue.

  YOU: **(a)**.. ?

  MAYA: Let's say 6 o'clock.

  YOU: **(b)**.. ?

  MAYA: We could meet at the bus stop.

  YOU: **(c)** .... ?

  MAYA: OK. Good idea. We'll meet at the restaurant.

  YOU: **(d)**.. .

  MAYA: See you there.

Now listen to Track 5.2 and respond when it's your turn.

Pronunciation: vowel sounds /e/ and /eɪ/

10 Listen to Track 5.3 and write /e/ or /eɪ/ according to the vowel sound you hear.

  a _/e/_ .... _check_ ....

  b ....

  c ....

  d ....

  e ....

  f ....

  g ....

  h ....

  i ....

  j ....

  k ....

Now listen again and write the word on the line.

11 Practise saying the words with the correct pronunciation.

➠ see 9B in the Mini-grammar

12 Read Mark's directions below and draw a line on the map to show the way to his house.

13 Now look at the route (in red) to Katie's house and write how to get there.

....

....

....

....

....

....

....

....

....

....

....

MARK: Walk along the road until you get to the bridge. Walk over the bridge and then turn left. Go down the hill towards the park. Go into the park and walk towards the lake. Turn right at the lake and walk towards the street. Turn right and walk down the hill. Turn onto Market Street and my house is the first house on the left.

How did you do?

14 Can you translate these sentences into your language?

a She stared at the man and then looked away.

....

b There's a tunnel under this street.

....

c My brother's at the office.

....

d What's the best time to meet?

....

e Have you got any suggestions?

....

f You have to go over the bridge.

....

g You have to drive up the hill and then turn left.

....

h Drive along this road for two miles.

....

15 Evaluation of Just learning in Unit 5

Answer these questions about the Just learning section in Unit 5 page 42 of the Student's Book.

Listening for specific information

When would you use *listening for specific information*? Tick the boxes below.

▪ At the airport you are listening to find out when your flight leaves.

▪ You are listening to the news to get the general idea about a story.

▪ You are listening to your friend telling you about her / his day.

▪ You are listening to the radio and you want to know the name of the singer of a song you heard.

Write one example of your own.

....
....
....
....
....
....

How easy is *listening for specific information* for you?

Very easy				Difficult
5	4	3	2	1

16 Phonetics

Look at the phonemic symbols on page 96. Write these words from Unit 5 in normal spelling.

a /ˈsteɪʃən/   _station_

b /ˈferi/   ....

c /bʌs/   ....

d /treɪn/   ....

e /pleɪn/   ....

f /ˈeskəleɪtə/   ....

Listen to Track 5.4 to check your answers and then read the words aloud.

Study grammar: the past simple

➞ see 8A in the Mini-grammar

1 Read the text. Fill in the blanks with the past simple of the verbs in brackets.

Sigmund Freud
a very short biography.

Sigmund Freud was born on May 6, 1856 in Freiberg (now Pribor, Slovakia). But he (**a**) *did not live* (not live) in Freiberg for long. When he (**b**) .... (be) four, his family (**c**) .... (move) to Vienna, Austria.

He (**d**) .... (live) in Vienna most of his life. He moved to England in 1938, after the Nazi invasion.

Sigmund Freud (**e**) .... (have) two much older half-brothers (from his father's first marriage) and seven brothers and sisters.

At 17, Freud (**f**) .... (start) university. He (**g**) .... (study) medicine. He (**h**) .... (graduate) from the University of Vienna and became a doctor. But he (**i**) .... (not like) medicine. He (**j**) .... (be) interested in people with emotional problems.

In 1886, Freud (**k**) .... (marry) Martha Bernays. They had six children.

Freud worked with Josef Breuer. In 1895 they published a book, *Studies in Hysteria*. It was about a 'talking cure' they (**l**) .... (use) with their patients. It was the beginning of psychoanalysis.

Freud's work is still very important today.
Sigmund Freud (**m**) .... (die) in London in 1939.

2 Complete the questions about Sigmund Freud for these answers.

a Where *did the Freud family move to* in 1860?
To Vienna.

b When ....
.... ?
When he was four.

c Where ....
.... go to school?
In Vienna.

d When ....
.... ?
In 1938.

e How many ....
.... ?
Nine, including his older half-brothers.

f Who ....
.... ?
Martha Brenays.

g Where ....
.... ?
In London, in 1939.

Study vocabulary: life stages

3 Read the text in Exercise 1 again. Find and copy phrases related to:

a birth _was born on_

b education ....

....

c marriage ....

d work ....

e death ....

4 Listen to Track 6.1. Answer the questions about yourself. Write full answers in the spaces.

a _My name's_ ....

b ....

c ....

d ....

e ....

f ....

5 Word Bank

Copy the chart below into your Word Bank notebook. Write the verbs and phrases in the box in the correct places in your chart. Make sure you write the whole phrase.

> to marry someone ◆ to be born ◆
> to be in love with (someone) ◆ to die ◆
> to fall in love with (someone) ◆
> to start school/university ◆
> to be keen on (someone) ◆ to be dead
> to love (someone) ◆
> to graduate from school/university ◆
> to have a baby ◆ to get married

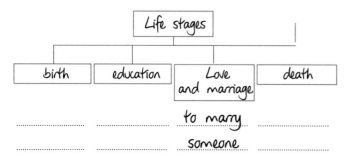

When you find other phrases, add them to the chart.

Study pronunciation: intonation (exclamations)

6 Listen to Track 6.2 and repeat these exclamations with the correct intonation.

a How nice!
b How awful!
c How funny!
d How boring!
e How exciting!

7 Listen to Track 6.3. After the beep, use an exclamation from Activity 6 to react to what the speakers say.

a FRIEND: I have to work on Saturday.

YOU: _How boring_ !

b FRIEND: My grandfather fell and broke his leg.

YOU: .... !

c FRIEND: I'm going to Australia!

YOU: .... !

d FRIEND: Ryan got married in a Superman suit!

YOU: .... !

e FRIEND: Look, I bought you an ice cream.

YOU: .... !

Study Grammar: *used to*

➡ see 8C in the Mini-grammar

8 Write sentences from this paragraph under the correct headings.

Believe it or not, I used to play in a rock band! We used to play at parties and clubs. Then I got married so I left the band. I used to miss playing terribly. But I don't anymore. Now, I usually play my guitar just at family parties.

Past habits

a *I used to play in a rock band!*

b ....

....

c ....

Present habits

d ....

....

Completed actions

e ....

....

9 Put the words and phrases in the correct order to make sentences about fashions. Add *used to* or *didn't use to* in the correct places, and put in any necessary capital letters.

Did you know?

a until the 1960s / British businessmen / wear / bowler hats / . /
British businessmen used to wear bowler hats until the 1960s.

b some ancient Romans / wash / very often / their hair / . / they / on 13 August, / it / only / wash / the birthday of the goddess Diana / . /

....

c their worst enemy / the ancient Egyptians / the picture of / paint / . inside their sandals / . /

....

d in the 1970s / egg, butter or toothpaste / punks / in their hair / put / . / they/ painted it / with food colouring or spray paint / then / . /

....

e in the 19th century / very tight corsets / women / wear / to look thin / . / faint / some women / or break their ribs / . /

....

10 Ask questions about the fashions in Exercise 9. Use the correct form of *used to*.

a What *did British businessmen use to wear* ?
Bowler hats.

b How often .... ?
Only once a year!

c Why... ?
Because then they could walk on them all the time, I suppose.

d When .... ?
On 13 August, the birthday of the goddess Diana.

e Why... ?
Because their corsets were too tight.

11 Write Bernie's part in the dialogue. Use comments and exclamations from the box. You will not need them all.

> Let me guess! You lost your mobile phone again, right? ◆
> Oh, no! ◆ That's nice. ◆ Uh, oh. ◆ That sounds familiar! ◆
> How stupid! ◆ I know the feeling. So, buy her more flowers.

ALEX: I did something really stupid.

BERNIE: (a) *Let me guess! You lost your mobile phone again, right?* ?

ALEX: No, no. I'm seeing Paula tonight, right? So I bought her some flowers.

BERNIE: (b) ....

ALEX: Yeah. But I put the flowers on the roof of the car, you know, to open the door.

BERNIE: (c) ....

ALEX: And I drove away with the flowers on the roof. Now I feel really stupid.

BERNIE: (d) ....

ALEX: I don't have money for the cinema <u>and</u> more flowers.

BERNIE: (e) ....

Listen to Track 6.4 to check your answers.

12 Listen to Track 6.5. You are Bernie. Read out his words when it's your turn.

13 Follow the instructions in *italics* to write a new dialogue. Use the dialogue in Exercise 11 to help you.

YOUR FRIEND: I did something really stupid.
(You think she lost her glasses again.)

YOU: *Let me guess!* ....
....

YOUR FRIEND: No. I bought a cake for my sister's birthday.
(You think that's kind.)

YOU: ....
....

YOUR FRIEND: But I put it on my chair and I sat on it!
(You think that was stupid. Advise her/him to buy another cake.)

YOU: ....
.... !

YOUR FRIEND: I haven't got any money!
(You have the same problem!)

YOU: ....
.... !

Listen to Track 6.6 to check your answers.

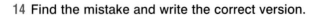

How did you do?

14 Find the mistake and write the correct version.

wrong	right
a Where you went on Sunday?	*Where did you go on Sunday?*
b What did you did yesterday?	
c I did no go with him.	
d Who you saw?	
e We no used to go to the beach.	
f Who use to play with guns?	
g I didn't used to like fish.	
h I use to have lunch with my family everyday now.	

15 Evaluation of Just learning in Unit 6

Answer these questions about the Just learning section in Unit 6 page 50, of the Student's Book.

> Using <u>everything</u> you know for listening
>
> **Which of these things do you do to help you understand when you listen? Tick the boxes below.**
>
> ▢ Thinking about what kind of listening it is (an advertisement, a conversation, etc.).
>
> ▢ Thinking about the situation.
>
> ▢ Listening to noises to know the situation.
>
> ▢ Turning up the volume really loud.
>
> ▢ Thinking about what I want to find out.
>
> **Write another example of what you do when you listen.**
>
> ....
> ....
> ....
> ....
> ....
>
> **How easy is listening for you?**
>
> | Very easy | | | | Difficult |
> |---|---|---|---|---|
> | 5 | 4 | 3 | 2 | 1 |

16 Phonetics

Look at the phonemic symbols on page 96. Write these words from Unit 6 in normal spelling.

a /ˈmeməri/   ....

b /ˈmæriːd/   ....

c /bɜːθ/   ....

d /deθ/   ....

e /ˈlʌvli/   ....

f /ˈjuːstuː/   ....

g /rəˈmembə/   ....

🎧 Listen to Track 6.7 to check your answers and then read the words aloud.

UNIT 7 | Time off

Study grammar: *-ing* nouns (gerunds)

➡ see 6A in the Mini-grammar

1 Label the pictures with the names of the sports. Which two sports are not Olympic sports?

> bowling ◆ cycling ◆ fencing ◆ life saving ◆ pistol shooting ◆
> rowing ◆ running ◆ show jumping ◆ swimming ◆ weightlifting

a *cycling*

f ....

b ....

g ....

c ....

h ....

d ....

i ....

e ....

j ....

2 Which five sports are part of a pentathlon? Complete the text with the names of the sports.

The Pentathlon

The modern pentathlon is an Olympic sport. It consists of competition in five events in one day:

(1) ....
(4.5 millimetre air pistol),

(2) ....
(free style – 200 metres),

(3) ....
(cross country – 3 kilometres),

(4) ....
(a course on horseback jumping over low walls and other obstacles) and

(5) ....
(indoor on a 18 x 2 metre piste).

3 Make the verbs into *-ing* nouns to complete the sentences.

a I love *watching* (watch) the Olympic Games on television.

b I need to go .... (shop) for food.

c .... (smoke) is bad for you so don't even start!

d .... (swim) in the sea is usually fun.

e Do you enjoy .... (buy) clothes?

f What do you think about .... (box) for women?

Study vocabulary: activities (and where we do them)

4 Complete each sentence with all the correct possibilities from the list.

a Do you want to go _bowling/sailing/skating_ ?
bowling sailing skating
listening to a concert

b Do you want to go .... ?
swimming shopping cycling watching a film

c Andy **came** .... with us.
dancing having fun rowing bowling

d Jan didn't want to **go to** ....
football baseball practice shopping riding

e Do you like **riding** .... ?
skates horses motorcycles a bicycle

f Matt can **play** ....
very well.
football golf boxing music

5 Word Bank

Make a chart like this in your Word Bank notebook. Write the activity words from Exercise 4 beside the correct verb in the chart. Can you add any other partners for each verb?

Activity verbs and their partners	
verbs	partners
go	swimming, shopping
come	
go to	
ride	
play	

6 Match the columns. Then use the words to complete the conversations.

golf   court
boxing   pitch
tennis   field
pool   ring
baseball   course
football   table
bowling   alley

a Where can we play tennis?
There's a _tennis court_ near my house.

b Why are there only 21 players on the
(..................) .... ?
The referee sent one player off.

c The fight is about to begin. The boxers are
already in the (..................) ....

d How many holes are there in this ....
.... ?
Only nine.

e Is bowling popular here?
Not yet. But they're building a ....
.... in the shopping centre.

f Does San Fernando have a baseball team?
We have a team but we play in San Diego:
there is no .... in
San Fernando.

g The hotel has three .... in the
games room.

7 Listen to Track 7.1. Number the words in the order you hear them.

bingo [1]
sung [ ]
drink [ ]
swimming [ ]
fun [ ]
thin [ ]
no [ ]
thing [ ]
sound [ ]
think [ ]
sun [ ]
thanks [ ]

8 Read the words in Exercise 7 aloud. Write them under the correct sound.

/n/	/ŋ/
fun	bingo

Which sound can go at the beginning, in the middle and at the end of words, and which sound is never at the beginning?

9 Listen to Track 7.2. Check your answers and repeat the words.

Study functions: inviting

10 Listen to Track 7.3 and fill in this chart.

What do the people invite their friends to do? Write the places or activities in the chart.

Do their friends say *yes*, *no*, or are they *not sure*? Tick the correct boxes in the chart.

people	place/activity	yes	no	not sure
1 Jamie invites Nat	bowling		✓	
2 Sue invites Sam	a b			
3 Tricia invites Mike	a b			

11 Listen to Track 7.3 again and add to the chart in Exercise 10. Write the expressions they use in the correct boxes.

people	place/activity	yes	no	not sure
1 Jamie invites Nat	bowling Would you like to come bowling?		I'd love to but I can't	

12 Use the expressions in the chart to invite Mike to the places in brackets. Then listen to Track 7.4 and say your lines after the beep.

YOU: (a dance) .... ?

MIKE: A dance? Well, I don't really like dancing.

YOU: (a concert) .... on Tuesday then?

MIKE: I'd love to but I'm busy on Tuesday.

YOU: (to dinner) .... tomorrow ?

MIKE: Now you're talking! Everybody says you're a great cook!

Study grammar: verb + -ing and verb + to + infinitive

➡ see 12E in the Mini-grammar

13 Read the text. Underline the correct verbs. Be careful, sometimes both verbs are possible.

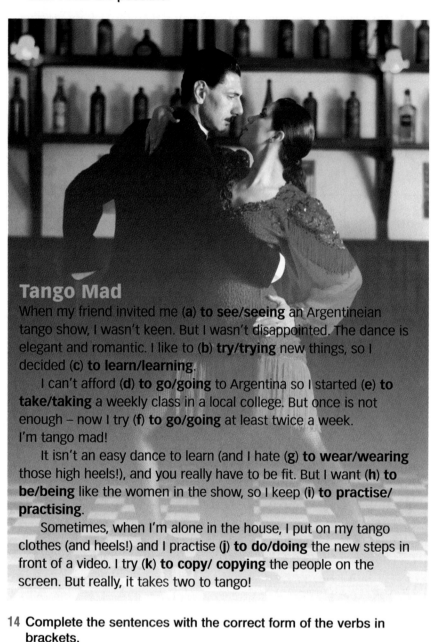

Tango Mad

When my friend invited me (**a**) **to see/seeing** an Argentineian tango show, I wasn't keen. But I wasn't disappointed. The dance is elegant and romantic. I like to (**b**) **try/trying** new things, so I decided (**c**) **to learn/learning**.

I can't afford (**d**) **to go/going** to Argentina so I started (**e**) **to take/taking** a weekly class in a local college. But once is not enough – now I try (**f**) **to go/going** at least twice a week. I'm tango mad!

It isn't an easy dance to learn (and I hate (**g**) **to wear/wearing** those high heels!), and you really have to be fit. But I want (**h**) **to be/being** like the women in the show, so I keep (**i**) **to practise/ practising**.

Sometimes, when I'm alone in the house, I put on my tango clothes (and heels!) and I practise (**j**) **to do/doing** the new steps in front of a video. I try (**k**) **to copy/ copying** the people on the screen. But really, it takes two to tango!

14 Complete the sentences with the correct form of the verbs in brackets.

a No, thank you. I really dislike ____dancing____ (dance).

b Don't forget .... (revise) your vocabulary!

c Mark promised .... (help) Cecilia with her project.

d Did you finish .... (write) the invitations?

e Imagine .... (go) to Argentina to learn the tango!

f Stop .... (talk) so loudly, please. I can't hear the film.

g I asked him to stop but he continued .... (talk).

h Yes, please! I love .... (go) on picnics.

15 What do you say in these situations? Write sentences using verbs from Exercise 14.

a You're having a party. Your friend said "I can help with the cooking". Now he's watching the football.
Don't forget to help with the cooking!

b Your friend was writing a report. You are not sure she has finished (it). What do you ask your friend?

c You're in a concert. The person behind you is talking on a mobile phone.

d Your friend has a grammar test tomorrow. What do you tell your friend?

e Someone invites you to see a horror movie. You strongly dislike horror movies.

How did you do?

16 Can you translate these sentences into your language?

a Do you want to come bowling?

....

b Smoking is very bad for you.

....

c I think watching movies is boring.

....

d I like walking in the park.

....

e What do you like doing in your spare time?

....

f Sailing, running and cycling are Olympic sports.

....

g My brother enjoys riding motorcycles.

....

h He promised to come to the party.

....

17 Evaluation of Just learning in Unit 7
Answers these questions about the Just learning section in Unit 7 page 56

Working together

What are the advantages of *working together*? Tick the boxes below.

▪ You have more chance to practise your English.

▪ You may learn things you didn't know from your partner.

▪ You may feel more confident than when you work alone.

▪ You can joke around even if you don't do any work.

▪ You can do things faster if you work with others.

Can you remember the last time you *worked with someone else*? How was your work, better or worse?

....

....

....

....

How easy is *working together* for you?

Very easy				Difficult
5	4	3	2	1

18 Phonetics

Look at the phonemic symbols on page 96. Write these words in normal spelling.

a /ˈbəʊlɪŋ/ ....

b /ˈleʒə/ ....

c /ɪnˈvaɪtɪŋ/ ....

d /laɪkˈmaɪndɪd/ ....

e /ˈaɪənɪŋ/ ....

f /ˈlɪsənɪŋ/ ....

g /ˈkɒnfɪdənt/ ....

h /kriːeɪˈtɪvɪti/ ....

Listen to Track 7.5 to check your answers and then read the words aloud.

Study vocabulary: feelings

1 Write sentences to react to the information. Use words from the chart.

be feel	very probably really	angry excited frightened happy jealous nervous proud sad

a A: My cat died!
   B: I'm sorry. *you're probably feeling very sad*.

b A: Thomas has a job interview tomorrow.
   B: _____ .

c A: Dave won the writing competition.
   B: Lucky Dave! I bet _____
   _____ .

d A: Adam and Kate are getting married.
   B: Really? I'm sure _____
   _____ .

e A: Penny's doing her first bungee jump in a minute!
   B: She _____
   _____ .

f A: Ian accidentally deleted all my work on the computer.
   B: Poor you! You _____
   _____ .

g A: Gina's going out with Laura's ex-boyfriend.
   B: Laura _____
   _____ .
   She's still in love with him.

h A: Millie is going to see Madonna in concert.
   B: _____
   _____ .
   Madonna's her favourite singer.

2 Match the nouns with the adjectives in the same word family.

nouns	adjectives
happiness	amused
sadness	angry
nervousness	disappointed
excitement	excited
amusement	frightened
disappointment	happy
anger	jealous
pride	nervous
jealousy	proud
fear	sad

Can you find two common endings for nouns in the chart?

3 Look at the picture. How do the people feel? Why do they feel that way? How are their bodies reacting? Write two sentences.

In picture a, *the people are feeling really* _____ *because they are* _____
_____
_____

In picture b, _____
_____
_____
_____

4 Word Bank

a Write the adjectives in this section in your Word Bank notebook. Write the situations in Exercise 1 to help you remember their meaning.

> To be / to feel sad
> e.g. when your cat dies.
>
> To be / to feel excited
> e.g. when you are going to see your favourite singer.

b Add other situations that are meaningful to you personally.

Study grammar: the past continuous

➠ see 8B in the Mini-grammar

5 Look at the picture carefully. What happened at seven o'clock yesterday morning? Choose the correct answer.

a A van crashed into a gorilla.
b A van crashed into another car.
c A gorilla escaped from a van.
d A gorilla went for breakfast.

6 Look at the picture again. What were the people doing at seven o'clock yesterday morning? Complete each sentence with the correct form of a verb from the box.

> clean ◆ stand ◆ have breakfast ◆ bring in ◆ deliver ◆ walk (x2) ◆ wait ◆ read ◆ jog

a A window cleaner *was cleaning a shop window* .

b A man .... his dog.

c A group of children ....

d Three people ....

e A boy .... on his bike.

f A man .... at the corner.

g A woman .... the milk.

h Two girls ....

i The baker ....

j Some people .... in a café.

7 Use these words to make questions in the past continuous. Use capital letters where necessary.

a window cleaner / do / what

What was the window cleaner doing .... ?

b you / do / at seven o'clock / yesterday morning

.... ?

c stand / the man / where

.... ?

d the people / wait for / what

.... ?

e the children / go / where

.... ?

f the girls / look at / what

.... ?

g the gorilla / walk / in the street / why

.... ?

8 Do not look at the picture in Exercise 6. Mark these sentences T (true) or F (false). Then correct the false statements.

a The man at the corner was reading a book.

F He wasn't reading a book, he was reading a newspaper .

b Everybody was looking at the gorilla.

....

....

c A woman was bringing in the newspaper.

....

....

d The children were riding their bikes to school.

....

....

e The baker was standing outside his shop.

....

....

f A man was walking a large dog.

....

....

g The children were wearing jeans.

....

....

9 Listen to Track 8.1. Notice strong and weak stress. Mark the words in italics S (strong) or W (weak).

a A: *Was* [S] the test difficult?
B: No. It *was* [W] nice *and* [ ] easy.

b A: *Can* [ ] you come and help?
B: Yes, I *can* [ ]. But I *can* [ ] only stay for an hour.

c A: How *was* [ ] your holiday?
B: Jamaica *was* [ ] hot *and* [ ] humid!
A: But *was* [ ] it nice?
B: Oh, it *was* [ ] beautiful – *and* [ ] a lot of fun!

10 Listen to Track 8.2. Read B's responses with the correct stress when it is your turn.

Study grammar: past continuous and past simple

→ see 8A and 8B in the Mini-grammar

11 Read the article. Complete the sentences with a correct form of the past simple or the past continuous of the verbs in brackets.

Smile! It's a lovely day

It was a lovely morning. When I left the house the sun (a) was shining (shine) and I (b) .... (feel) happy. But the feeling didn't last long. When I (c) .... (arrive) at the station, lots of people were waiting to buy a ticket. The man (d) .... (close) his ticket window just as I got there. 'Sorry. It's my tea break,' he said.

The train was leaving when I (e) .... (get) to the platform. The next train was packed. I (f) .... (stand) all the way while some children sat comfortably. No one (g) .... (offer) me a seat. Children are so impolite these days!

A woman was standing next to me. She (h) .... (read) her paper when a child put his hand in her bag. 'Thief!' I shouted. 'That boy is taking your purse!' But the boy was the woman's son. Well, I (i) .... only .... (try) to help.

When I left the station it (j) .... (rain). People were pushing and running. When I got to the office, I certainly (k) .... (not smile) anymore.

12 Read the article again. Find sentences to match the patterns.

Past simple – happened
Past continuous – was happening
Pattern 1
Something was happening **when** something else happened.
a The train was leaving when I got to the platform .
b ....
c ....

Pattern 2
Something was happening **while/when** something else was happening.
d ....

Pattern 3
Something happened **while** something else was happening.
e ....
f ....
g ....

Pattern 4
Two things happened at the same time.
h ....

13 Complete the questions with the correct form of the verbs in brackets, past simple or past continuous.

a A: What __was__ Brian __doing__ when you __arrived__ ? (*do, arrive*)
B: He was washing his car.

A: What .... he .... when you .... ? (*do, arrive*)
B: He offered me a cup of tea.

b A: What .... you .... when you .... the accident? (*do, see*)
B: I was driving home.

A: What .... you .... when you .... the accident? (*do, see*)
B: I phoned an ambulance.

c A: What .... you .... about when the alarm clock .... ? (*dream, ring*)
B: I was dreaming of you.

A: What .... you .... when the alarm clock .... ? (*do, ring*)
B: I threw it out of the window!

d A: What .... your friend .... when you .... home? (*watch, get*)
B: A football game.

A: What .... you .... when you .... there? (*watch, be*)
B: The same football game!

14 Listen to Track 8.3. Match the conversations with the pictures.

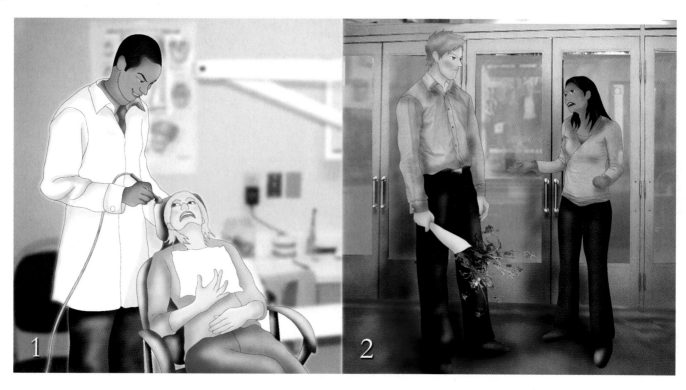

15 Listen to Track 8.3 again. Write the apologies in the spaces.

Conversation a

A: You're late!

B: _Sorry!_ ....

A: Well, we said 8 o'clock and it's 8.45 now.

B: I know. ....

A: It wasn't much fun, you know?

B: ....

I lost my laptop. That's why I'm late.

A: Oh, I'm really sorry. ....

Listen, do you still want to see the film?

Conversation b

A: Good afternoon, Mr Rice. ....

B: Yes, I see your appointment was at 4.

A: .... There was a lot of traffic.

B: Well, never mind. Now, open wide please.

A: Ouch!

B: Oops, ... Did that hurt?

16 Listen again to Conversation a on Track 8.4. You are B.
Respond when it's your turn.

How did you do?

17 Find the mistake and write the correct version.

wrong	right
a Was you calling me?	Were you calling me?
b I having a shower when you called.	
c It start raining while Josh was playing tennis.	
d Josh was running when it was starting to rain.	
e What did he did when he saw you?	
f She apologised for break my mobile.	
g Everybody were having fun.	
h How many people was waiting to buy a ticket?	

18 Evaluation of Just learning in Unit 8

Answer these questions about the Just learning section in Unit 8 page 63 of the Student's Book.

Classifying words

Which of these things can *classifying words in families* help you with? Tick the boxes below.

▨ to guess new words

▨ to speak better

▨ to understand how words are formed

▨ to remember words

Write one idea of your own.

....

....

....

....

How easy is it for you to *classify* words?

Very easy   Difficult

   5   4   3   2   1

19 Phonetics.

Look at the phonemic symbols on page 96. Write these words from Unit 8 in normal spelling.

a /ə'pɒlədʒaɪz/ ....

b /'sɒri/ ....

c /'smaɪlɪŋ/ ....

d /'evrɪbɒdi/ ....

e /'dʒeləs/ ....

f /'wʌri/ ....

Listen to Track 8.5 to check your answers and then read the words aloud.

UNIT 9 Can you do it?

Study grammar: can and can't

→ see 5A in the Mini-grammar

1 Match the sentences with the meanings.

a Abilities   1 Can you meet me after class?
b Know   2 Can you print this for me
  how to   please?
c Possibility   3 Can you use this software?
d Request   4 Can you type without looking
                       at the keyboard?

2 Rewrite these sentences using can or can't.

a With this new software it is possible to design posters but it is not possible to make them in colour.

  With this new software you can design posters, but you can't make them in colour. .

b Do you know how to download music from the Internet?

  ....
  .... ?

c Please help me with this programme.

  ....
  .... ?

d Is it possible to take photos with this mobile?

  ....
  .... ?

e Rizwan is good at taking photos of plants.

  ....
  ....

f I know how to fix a computer quickly.

  ....
  ....

g Howa is definitely not good at mixing music.

  ....
  ....

h Please take the CD out of the machine.

  ....
  .... ?

Study vocabulary: phrasal verbs

3 Match the beginning of the sentences in column 1 with the correct ending in column 2.

column 1	column 2
a Switch off	1 the volume. I can't hear anything.
b Put on	2 the phone. I'm busy.
c Turn up	3 the light when you go.
d Turn on	4 the printer before you use it.
e Turn off	5 the TV. The programme is starting!
f Plug in	6 the computer when you finish.
g Pick up	7 the headset. We don't want to listen to your music.

4 Rewrite the sentences you made in Exercise 3, changing the place of the preposition.

a _Switch the computer off._

b ....

c ....

d ....

e ....

f ....

g ....

5 Complete these sentences with a phrasal verb from Exercise 3.

a Please ...*turn down*... the volume. It's too high.

b Did you remember to .... the DVD player when you left?

c Why don't you .... the lamp. It's too dark here.

d Of course the radio doesn't work – you didn't

  ....

e .... your coat. It's cold out there!

f You don't have to .... this radio. It's got batteries.

g Can you .... the answering machine? I want to listen to my messages.

6 Word Bank

Phrasal verbs

Make boxes like these in your Word Bank notebook. Write a phrasal verb from this unit in each box, with the words to go with it. Note any special grammar too.

switch off
the computer
your walkman
special grammar
switch the computer off.

put on
your coat
special grammar

Add as many words as you can to each box.

➠ see 5B in the Mini-grammar

7 Mark the sentences 1 or 2, depending on their meaning.

> **Meanings**
> 1 talking about abilities in the past.
> 2 talking about things that were difficult to do but you did.

a Jim could climb up palm trees when he was young.   ....

b Kris managed to open a window and got into the house.   ....

c Did you manage to solve the puzzle?   ....

d They couldn't fix Maria's MP3 player.   ....

8 Read the text. Underline the correct verbs.

Kids these days can do things I **(a) could/couldn't/managed to/didn't manage to** do at their age. Some things I still can't do. I feel a bit silly sometimes.

Yesterday I wanted to download some music. I **(b) could/couldn't/managed to/didn't manage to** find the correct website but **(c) could/couldn't/managed to/didn't manage to** put it onto my MP3 player. My eight-year-old daughter was watching, amused. Later she asked 'Did you manage to put your music onto your MP3 player, dad?' 'Yes,' I said. 'I **(d) could/couldn't/managed to/didn't manage to** do it perfectly well, thank you.'

I read the manual again but I still **(e) could/couldn't/managed to/didn't manage to** understand anything. In the end I had to ask her to help. She did it in a minute. But then she **(f) could/couldn't/managed to/didn't manage to** use a computer at five and she **(g) could/couldn't/managed to/didn't manage to** record programmes on TV at six. As for the Internet, she **(h) could/couldn't/managed to/didn't manage to** use it for homework ages ago.

It's amazing, isn't it? But she **(i) could/couldn't/managed to/didn't manage to** learn the arithmetic times tables until yesterday. Hey, what's eight times six?

9 Complete the sentences. Use *could*, *couldn't*, *managed to* or *didn't manage to*.

a Last night I finally ...managed to... get to Level six of this game!

b .... you use a computer when you were ten?

c When Kevin was at school, he .... spell, but now he can.

d I phoned Jean lots of times but I .... speak to her. She's never in!

e Irene lost some computer files and she .... get them back. She was really upset.

f She .... type with her eyes shut in those days.

g Vanessa .... understand the instructions at all.

h Did they .... install the new software?

i Can you believe it? Johnny .... repair watches when he was five!

Study functions: making phone calls

10 Listen to Track 9.1.
Who can Ricky speak to, Jane, Larry, Lisa or Dr Lewis?
Why can't Ricky speak to the others? Write the reasons on the lines.

Dr Lewis. ....
....

Jane. ....
....

Ricky.

Lisa. ....
....

Larry. ....

11 Listen to Track 9.1 again. Write

a three ways of answering the phone:
<u>Hello? Eton Electronics (the name of the company)</u> .
....
....

b three ways to ask to speak to someone:
....
....
....

c an expression that means 'can you wait?'
....

12 Fill in the rest of the phone call. Then listen to Track 9.2 and read out your lines when it's your turn.

YOU: *(answering the phone)*

(a) Hello_____ .

FRANCES: Hi. This is Frances. Can I speak to Carmen, please?

YOU: *(say she is not in)*

(b) ....

....

FRANCES: When will she be back?

YOU: *(you are not sure – offer to take a message.)*

(c) ....

.... ?

FRANCES: Yes, please. Tell her Frances called. Can she meet me outside the cinema at 8.30, not at 8. I can't be there earlier.

YOU: *(read out the message)*

(d) ....

....

....

....

FRANCES: That's right. Who's speaking please?

YOU: *(say who you are)*

(e) ....

FRANCES: OK. Thanks for your help. Bye.

Study pronunciation: question intonation

13 Read the questions aloud. Does the voice go up or down at the end? Mark the intonation of the questions D (down) or U (up). Then listen to Track 9.3 to check your answers.

a Can I speak to Lila?   [U]
b Are you busy?   [   ]
c Do you want me to call later? [   ]
d When can I have it back?   [   ]
e What can I do for you?   [   ]
f How are you?   [   ]

14 Listen to Track 9.3 again. Repeat the questions after the beep with the correct intonation.

15 Choose questions from Exercise 13 to complete this conversation.

LILA: Hello?

YOU: (a) Can I speak to Lila ?

LILA: Speaking.

YOU: Hi, Lila. (b) .... ?

LILA: Fine, thanks.

YOU: (c) .... ?

LILA: Yes, actually. I am a little.

YOU: (d) .... ?

LILA: No, that's OK. What can I do for you?

YOU: I really need my camera. (e) .... ?

LILA: Oh, right. Well, I have bad news for you.

Now listen to Track 9.4 and read out the questions with the correct intonation when it's your turn.

How did you do?

16 Can you translate these sentences into your language?

a Can you take photos with your mobile?...................................

....

b I can't put new software onto my computer. ....

....

c We can't take your call at the moment. ....

....

d Did you manage to fix your computer?..................................

....

e I couldn't help him. ....

....

....

f Could you use the Internet ten years ago?...............................

....

g Do you want me to say you called?......................................

....

....

h Would you like to hold? ....

....

....

i Can I speak to your mother?

....

....

j I'd rather buy a camcorder.

....

....

....

17 Evaluation of Just learning in Unit 9

Answer these questions about the Just learning section in Unit 9 page 72 of the Student's Book.

Words together (collocations)

Why is it a good idea to write *words together*? Tick the boxes below.

☐ Because I can then use the words correctly.

☐ Because it is easier to remember the words.

☐ Because some words have different meanings.

☐ Because it is easier to guess new vocabulary.

Write another reason of your own.

....

....

....

....

How often do you write *words and their collocations*?

Very often   Never

5	4	3	2	1

Go back and read the Just learning section in the Student's Book. How useful is this advice to you in your language learning?

Very useful   Not useful

5	4	3	2	1

18 Phonetics

Look at the phonemic symbols on page 96. Write these words from Unit 9 in normal spelling.

a /kaːnt/   *can't*

b /kuːdnt/ ....

c /kʊd/ ....

d /ˈmesɪdʒ/ ....

e /ˈmænədʒd/ ....

f /ˈbɪziː/ ....

Listen to Track 9.5 to check your answers and then read the words aloud.

UNIT 10 Give and take

Study grammar: verbs with two objects

➡ see 12F in the Mini-grammar

1 Read this paragraph and answer the questions below.

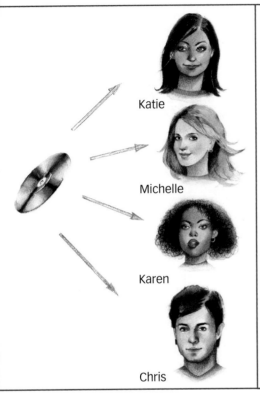

Katie

Michelle

Karen

Chris

Katie bought <u>a new CD</u>. She listened to it twice and then Michelle borrowed it. Michelle was showing it to Chris and she left it at his house. The next day, (Chris) asked Michelle if he could borrow it, because he liked it. After a week Katie asked Michelle to give the CD back to her. Michelle said, "I'm sorry, Katie, but I lent it to Chris." So Katie phoned Chris. "Yes, I borrowed it from Michelle," said Chris, "but then I bought the CD at the music shop." "So, who has my CD?" said Katie. "I gave it back to Michelle and then she lent it to Karen."

a What did Katie buy? ......*a CD*......

b How many times did she listen to it? ....

c Who did Katie lend it to? ....

d Whose house did Michelle leave it at? ....

e Who asked to borrow the CD? ....

f Who did he ask? ....

g When did Katie ask Michelle for the CD? ....

h What did Chris buy? ....

i Who did he give the CD to? ....

j Who borrowed the CD from Michelle? ....

2 Now underline the direct objects in the text, and circle the indirect objects.

3 Complete these sentences with a suitable word from the box.

> buy ◆ borrow ◆ leave ◆ lend ◆
> owe ◆ pay ◆ read ◆ send ◆
> show ◆ teach ◆ write

a Mum, will you ...*buy*...... me a new toy, please?

b Did you .... the money you .... to your sister?

c This is a letter to the manager. I'm .... it to him to complain about the hotel room.

d Will you .... me that book when you have .... it?

e I'd like to .... your car, if you don't mind.

f Come here and I'll .... you how to use this new computer program.

g Do you think you could .... me how to play the piano?

h He didn't want to .... his children alone with the new babysitter, because she seemed strange.

4 Match the word to the definition.

birthday ◆ Father's Day ◆
wedding ◆ Mother's Day ◆
engagement

a when two people get married
....wedding....

b when two people decide that
they want to get married

....

c the day you were born

....

d a day to celebrate women
who have children

....

e a day to celebrate men who
have children

....

5 Look at these pictures and complete the sentences. Use these words. You will need some of them more than once.

credit card ◆ receipt ◆ present ◆ wrap ◆ unwrap ◆
shop assistant ◆ show ◆ pay ◆ give ◆ birthday

a The ....shop assistant.... is ....showing.... the earrings
to Celina.

b The .... is .... the earrings.

c Celina is .... with a ....

d The .... is giving her a ....

e Celina is .... her mother a ....
for her ....

f Celina's mother is .... the ....

6 Word Bank

In your Word Bank notebook, make a list of all the different things you can give as presents for these occasions.

wedding	
engagement	
birthday	
Mother's Day	
Father's Day	

7 Put these words in the correct order to make sentences. Use capital letters where necessary.

1 just / I / wanted / it's / what / . /

It's just what I wanted.

you / I'm / it / like / glad / . /

....

2 all / you / for / help / your / thank / . /

....

....

welcome / you're / . /

....

3 party / success / a / you / to / thanks / the / great / was / . /

....

....

a / was / pleasure / it / . /

....

4 me / so / thanks / helping / homework / much / with / for / my / . /

....

....

....

....

problem / no / . /

....

5 for / thanks / lot / dinner / a / . /

....

it / mention / don't /. /

....

Now listen to Track 10.1 and check your answers.

8 Now match each dialogue in Exercise 7 with a picture. Write the numbers in the boxes.

9 Now imagine you are in these situations. Write what you would say.

a It's your birthday and your friend gave you a CD of your favourite band.

....

b It's your friend's birthday and he thanks you for the DVD that you gave.

....

c Your brother helped you to fix your bicycle.

....

d Your mother cooked you a delicious dinner.

....

Listen to Track 10.2 and speak when it's your turn.

Pronunciation: /θ/ and /ð/

🔊 **10** Listen to Track 10.3. Listen to each word and write the symbol of the sound that you hear.

<u>think</u> /θ/   <u>there</u> /ð/

a thank   /θ/
b with   ....
c that   ....
d three   ....
e north   ....
f mother   ....
g thirty   ....
h mouth   ....
i father   ....
j this   ....

11 Practise saying these sentences with the correct pronunciation of 'th', /θ/ or /ð/.

a Don't forget to thank your mother.
b Do you think he's thirty?
c This is my father.
d Don't put that in your mouth.
e There's the person who's from the north.

🔊 Listen to Track 10.4 and repeat the sentences with the same pronunciation.

Study grammar: verb + object + (to) + infinitiv

➡ see 11B and 12G in the Mini-grammar

12 Choose the correct form to complete these sentences.

a She let her son (play)/ to play in the sea.
b Maria warned him *not to fall / to not fall* in the river.
c Cristina told Jason *not to stay / not stay* very late.
d Laura and Frank invited them *to come / come* to dinner.
e Katie reminded her son *to cook / cook* the eggs for the picnic.
f We begged them *not to wait / not wait* too long.
g She wanted *to go / go to* the party.

13 Use an appropriate verb from Exercise 12 to write what they said. The first one is done for you.

a "Don't forget to take your books." Mary to Jake.
   Mary reminded Jake to take his books.

b "Would you like to come to dinner?" Ron and Jody to Kevin.

c "You have to go home now." Susie to Michelle and Claire.

d "Do you want to watch TV?" Chris to Mike.

e "Put it down now!" David to Janie.

f "That's dangerous. Don't go in there." Emma to Richie and Charles.

g "I'd like some cake." Ellie.

h "Please, please help me." Alice to Marty.

54 unit ten

How did you do?

14 Find the mistake and write the correct version.

wrong	right
a She gave a present Jane.	*She gave Jane a present.*
b They lent to him some money.	
c She paid in credit card.	
d The assistant wrapped down the present.	
e Thank you from all your help.	
f You welcome.	
g My mother let me to go to the party.	
h I told him to not wait for me.	

15 Evaluation of Just learning in Unit 10

Answer these questions about the Just learning section in Unit 10 page 78 of the Student's Book.

Finding and using 'rules'

Which of these things can *using grammar rules* help you with? Tick the boxes below.

- ▪ to speak more correctly
- ▪ to write more correctly
- ▪ to understand a conversation
- ▪ to understand how English works

Write one idea of your own.

....

....

....

How easy is it for you to *use grammar rules*?

Very easy				Difficult
5	4	3	2	1

Go back and read the Just learning section in the Student's Book. How useful is the advice about *finding and using rules* to you in your language learning?

Very useful				Not useful
5	4	3	2	1

16 Phonetics

Look at the phonemic symbols on page 96. Write these words from Unit 10 in normal spelling.

a /θæŋk/   thank ....

b /θɪŋk/   ....

c /send/   ....

d /əʊ/   ....

e /kæʃ/   ....

f /rəˈsiːt/   ....

g /ʌnˈræp/   ....

Listen to Track 10.5 to check your answers and then read the words aloud.

UNIT 11 Before I'm thirty?

Study grammar: the present perfect

➡ see 10C in the Mini-grammar

1 Match the question to the answer in this online interview.

a What unusual foods have you tried?
b What are your hobbies?
c When did you become a vegetarian?
d Which country did you like best?
e Can you tell us something about yourself?
f What countries have you visited?
g How long have you lived in London?
h When did you go there?

Q: 1 _Can you tell us something about yourself?_
A: My name is Nadia Burton. I'm 22 and I'm from London.

Q: 2 _____?
A: I've lived in London all my life, but I have travelled to a lot of different countries and done a lot of interesting things.

Q: 3 _____?
A: I've visited most countries in Europe, except Sweden, Norway and Denmark. I really want to go there.

Q: 4 _____?
A: My favourite country is the Czech Republic.

Q: 5 _____?
A: I went there in 2004 and I loved it.

Q: 6 _____?
A: I'm a travel agent, so travel is my job and my hobby. When I'm not travelling I like to cook. I love to try unusual food.

Q: 7 _____?
A: I have eaten a lot of unusual fruits and vegetables like star fruit, but there are a lot of meats that I have never eaten, because I am a vegetarian.

Q: 8 _____?
A: About five years ago. I haven't eaten meat for five years.

2 Complete these conversations with the present perfect or the past simple.

a MIKE: _Have_ you ever _eaten_ (eat) octopus?

LAURA: Yes, I _____ (try) it last year.

MIKE: _____ you _____ (like) it?

LAURA: Yes, it _____ (be) delicious.

b CINDY: I _____ (see) a great movie last night. It's called 'Escape from the Edge'. _____ you _____ (see) it?

BRAD: No, I _____ (not be) to the cinema for a long time, but I _____ (go) to the theatre last week.

CINDY: Really? What _____ you _____ (see)?

BRAD: It _____ (be) a play called 'A Merry Life'.

🔊 Now listen to Track 11.1 to check your answers.

Study vocabulary: performance

3 Complete the sentences with one of these words.

> review ◆ book ◆ curtain ◆ play ◆ performance ◆
> audience ◆ clapped ◆ stage

a I read a ......*review*...... of the movie. It said that the movie was excellent.

b Do we need to .... tickets?

c The actors were already on the .... when we arrived late.

d There was a huge .... at the theatre on opening night. There was not one empty seat.

e The .... went up at the beginning of the show and came down at the end.

f There's a .... in this theatre tonight and tomorrow there's a concert.

g The people watching .... for ten minutes at the end of the show.

h The actors were fantastic in the first .... of Shakespeare's 'Romeo and Juliet' last night.

4 Look at these movie posters. Then listen to the people on Track 11.2. talking about the movies and write which movie they are talking about.

a ....   b ....   c ....   d ....

5 Now imagine you saw the movies. Write here what you would say when your friend asks you:

a FRIEND: Have you seen 'Days of Laughter'?

YOU: ....

....

b FRIEND: Have you seen 'Night of the Zombie Killers'?

YOU: ....

....

c FRIEND: Have you seen 'The Long, Hot Summer'?

YOU: ....

....

d FRIEND: Have you seen 'The New York Race'?

YOU: ....

....

Now listen to Track 11.3 and answer when it's your turn.

6 Word Bank

Which of the words in this vocabulary section refer to movies, which to plays, and which to both?

Make a diagram like this in your Word Bank notebook and write the words in the right place.

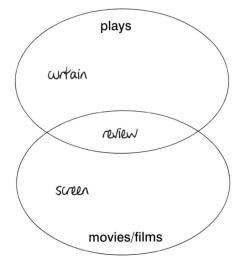

Study grammar: *for* and *since*

➠see 10D in the Mini-grammar

7 Complete these phrases with *for* or *since*.

a I've known him ....*for*........ four years.

b We've lived here .... I was a child.

c She waited for him .... twenty-five minutes.

d They've been married .... 1988.

e It's been three years .... I last saw her.

f I haven't been here .... we were both ten years old.

g She has been so worried about it .... you told her.

8 Read this paragraph and answer the questions below.

Hi! I'm Lydia Brown and I'm from London. I moved to Paris five years ago and I moved back to London three months ago. I'm an executive for a music company and I work long hours. I've worked in this job since 2000 and I love it. My hobbies are capoeira and dancing. I started classical ballet when I was little and I also do modern dance. I've never tried tap dancing, but I have always wanted to, ever since I was a child.

a How long did Lydia live in Paris? ...*for five years*...

b How long has she lived in London? ....

c How long has she been doing her present job? ....

d How long has she studied classical ballet? ....

e How long has she wanted to try tap dancing? ....

Study functions: booking tickets, tables, rooms

9 Put these two conversations in order.

a

a OK, Ms Healey. Next Wednesday at 8 o'clock, table for two.
b Just for two.
c Thank you very much.
d Jennifer Healey.
e Hello. I'd like to book a table, please.
f 8 pm? Right. And what's your name?
g Two people on Wednesday. OK, and what time were you thinking of?
h 8 o'clock.
i Murray's restaurant here.
j Next Wednesday, please.
k Sure. And how many people is that for?
l Certainly. What day is that for?

i ....

b

a Oh dear. What about tomorrow?
b Certainly, sir. Can I have your credit card number?
c Yes. It's 6475 7564 ......
d Two nights? Is that for tonight?
e OK, can I book that room, please?
f We have one room available tomorrow.
g Yes, tonight and tomorrow night.
h The Garden Hotel. Can I help you?
i Yes, I'd like a room for two nights, please.
j I'm afraid the hotel is full tonight.

h ....

🔊 Listen to Track 11.4 and check your answers.

10 Now listen to Track 11.5. Imagine you are the woman on the phone to the restaurant, and then the man in the hotel. You can change information if you want. Speak when it is your turn.

Pronunciation: stress and intonation to show feelings

11 Listen to Track 11.6 and circle what the speaker is feeling in each sentence.

a (happy) / sad
b tired / sad
c bored / angry
d happy / surprised
e angry / upset
f upset / bored
g surprised / tired

Repeat the sentences with the same stress and intonation.

12 Practise saying this sentence in all of the different ways you heard in Exercise 11.

I can't believe that he told you that.

How did you do?

13 Can you translate these sentences into your language?

a Have you ever won a competition?

b I've never failed an exam.

c At the end of the performance the audience clapped.

d That film was very scary.

e I've lived in my house for five years.

f I haven't seen a good film since February.

g I'd like to book a table.

h Is there anything else I can do for you?

i You didn't put it in your bag, did you?

j We're safe, aren't we?

14 Evaluation of Just learning in Unit 11

Answer these questions about the Just learning section in Unit 11 page 92 of the Student's Book.

Checking your work

Which of these things can *checking your work* help you with? Tick the boxes below.

▨ to find grammar mistakes

▨ to correct spelling mistakes

▨ to see if your writing is interesting

▨ to learn irregular verbs

▨ to see if your writing is clear

Write one idea of your own.

How easy is it for you to *check your own work*?

Very easy				Difficult
5	4	3	2	1

Go back and read the Just learning section in the Student's Book. How useful is the advice about *checking your work* to you in your language learning?

Very useful				Not useful
5	4	3	2	1

15 Phonetics

Look at the phonemic symbols on page 96. Write these words from Unit 11 in normal spelling.

a /'nevə/   never

b /'ɔːdɪjənts/

c /rə'hɜːs/

d /rə'læks/

e /klæp/

f /pə'fɔːməns/

g /sɪns/

h /'skeəriː/

i /'vaɪələnt/

j /'kredɪtkɑːd/

Listen to Track 11.7 to check your answers and then read the words aloud.

UNIT 12 Making a difference

Study vocabulary: word families

1 Read these paragraphs about two people and circle the correct blue words to complete them.

Shawn Fanning (born in 1980) was just 18 years old when he started 'Napster' – a way to share music files over the Internet for free – without paying. Fanning was a university student when he became a) interested / interesting / interest in the Internet. He left university to b) move / movement / moved to California and start his business.

Today Fanning owns a company called SNOCAP. This company c) protects / protection / protected the rights of people who write music – the opposite of his early days with Napster!

Arundhati Roy was born in 1961. She is a writer and d) active / activist from Bengal, India. Her first novel took her five years to write and it is called *The God of Small Things*.

Today Roy travels the world giving e) speak / spoken / speeches about the environment and justice and she is an f) inspire / inspiration to the people who meet her. She is g) marriage / marry / married to a film-maker and lives in Delhi.

2 Complete this word family table.

verb	noun	adjective
a —	scientist science	scientific
b discover	....	
c	....	interested (in)
d	destruction	....
e —	environment	....
f	plant	....
g protect	....	....
h	....	married
i move	....	....
j —	....	active

3 Use one of the words from Exercise 2 in each of the gaps in these sentences.

a My sister's favourite subject at school is __science__ and when she grows up she wants to be a ....

b An .... is someone who is interested in protecting the world.

c The .... of the rainforest is dangerous for the .... , because the rainforest affects the weather.

d It is important that we .... more trees in the world.

e The .... of radium was important for medicine.

f Many important .... in the world .... wild animals.

g The couple got .... last year. The .... took place at the beach.

4 Word Bank

Make a table like this in your Word Bank notebook.

Write ten word families that you know in the table.

verb	noun	adjective
rescue	rescuer	rescued

➠ see 4C in the Mini-grammar

5 Match what the person is saying to the pictures.

    a He won't be here. ....

    b I'll carry that for you. ....

    c I think you'll like this. ....

    d I think I'll go for a walk. ....

Which sentences are examples of predictions? ....

Which sentences are examples of unplanned decisions? ....

6 Complete this conversation with appropriate forms of the future simple.

RICHIE: Hey Emma! You know a lot about runners. Who

    a) ...will............... (win) the marathon on Saturday?

EMMA: Well, Mark Brown is the fastest man, so I think he

    b).............................. (get) first place.

RICHIE: What about Mike Harris? Do you think he

    c) .... (come) second?

EMMA: No, he **d)** .... (be) second. Fred Garrett is faster

    than he is. Fred **e)** .... (beat) Mike Harris.

RICHIE: **f)** .... the race .... (be) on TV, do

    you think?

EMMA: Oh, yes, I'm sure it **g)** .... (be) on TV, but I

    h) .... (be able) to watch it.

RICHIE: Why not?

EMMA: I **i)** .... probably .... (have to) help my
parents in their shop.

RICHIE: I **j)** .... (record) it for you and you can watch

    it later.

EMMA: Thanks.

7 Complete the conversations with these words. Use capital letters where necessary.

> can I ◆ would you like ◆ don't worry ◆
> allow me ◆ why don't ◆ would be ◆ sure ◆
> don't worry ◆ can you ◆ how about

a A: ..Would you like.. me to help you with dinner?

  B: Thanks. That .... great.

  .... chop those onions?

b A: You look tired. .... if I make you a nice cup of tea?

  B: .... , dear, but I'm fine. I'll have some tea later.

c A: I can't open this door.

  B: .... It is very heavy.

d A: .... you do the first part of the reading and I'll do the second part? So we save time.

  B: .... It's about 100 pages altogether.

e A: .... help you to do the shopping?

  B: .... about it. I only need to get a few things.

Now listen to Track 12.1 and check your answers.

8 Complete the conversations for these situations.

a Would you like me to help you, son?

....

....

....

b Wow! What a mess! How about if we help you to get the room ready?

....

....

....

Now listen to Track 12.2 and speak when it's your turn.

9 Listen to these pairs of sentences on Track 12.3 and write the number of the sentence that you hear.

A You have to say 'goodbye'. ......
You have to say 'good boy'. **1**

B Can I look at that tie? ......
Can I look at that toy? ......

C Be careful! Don't slip on the oil. ......
Be careful! Don't slip in the aisle. ......

D Would you like to try? ......
Would you like to, Troy? ......

10 Now match these contexts to the sentences. Write the sentence number from Exercise 9.

a A young child who is at a friend's house wants to play with his friend's toy. **B2**

b A person is telling someone how to train a dog. ....

c A young man is asking his friend Troy if he wants to go to the movies with him. ....

d A young person has a new video game that he wants his friend to play. ....

e A man in a shop wants to buy a new tie. ....

f A mother is talking to her young son who doesn't want to go home. ....

g There is oil on the road and a mother warns her daughter. . ...

h It has been raining on a ship and the aisles (where people walk) are wet. ....

Study grammar: probability modals

➡ see 5C in the Mini-grammar

11

Look at the picture. Who will arrive home first?

Complete these sentences with one of these verb forms.

will ◆ might ◆ may ◆ could ◆ won't

a I think Ellie ....

b Matt ....

c Charlie ....

d Alice ....

e Kevin ....

12 Look at these pictures. Write three sentences about what you think the pictures could, might or may be part of.

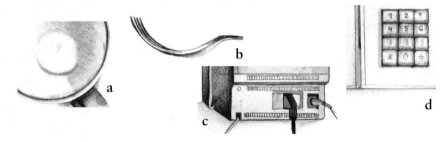

a This could be a plate.
....
....

b ....
....
....

c ....
....
....

d ....
....
....

Look at the answers in the Answer key booklet to see if you were right.

How did you do?

13 Find the mistake and write the correct version.

wrong	right
a I'm very interesting in this book.	I'm very interested in this book.
b She got marry last year.	
c I want to be a biology when I grow up.	
d I think he'll to win the race.	
e Are you sure he willn't be at home?	
f Will I being rich?	
g Will you like some help with your homework?	
h How about if I making you a sandwich?	
i I'm sure John might win the race.	
j Susan could got the prize.	

14 Evaluation of Just learning in Unit 12

Answer these questions about the Just learning section in Unit 12 page 95 of the Student's Book.

Scanning

When would you *scan* a text? Tick the boxes below.

- ▢ You want to know the times of a film in the newspaper.
- ▢ You are looking for important dates and names in a text.
- ▢ You are looking for the weather in your country on the Internet.
- ▢ You want to know the meaning of a word.
- ▢ You are looking for a phone number in the phone book.

Can you remember the last time you *scanned* a text? Why did you *scan* it?

....

....

How easy is *scanning* for you?

Very easy   Difficult

   5   4   3   2   1

Go back and read the Just learning section in the Student's Book. How useful is the advice about *scanning* to you in your language learning?

Very useful   Not useful

   5   4   3   2   1

15 Phonetics

Look at the phonemic symbols on page 96. Write these words from Unit 12 in normal spelling.

a /spiːtʃ/   speech

b /ˈplɑːntəd/   ....

c /wəʊnt/   ....

d /θæŋks/   ....

e /klaʊn/   ....

f /kləʊn/   ....

g /meɪ/   ....

h /maɪt/   ....

Listen to Track 12.4 to check your answers and then read the words aloud.

Study functions: asking for language help

1 Complete the conversation below with one of these words or expressions. You will need to use some words more than once.

> mean ◆ say ◆ what's ◆ call ◆ means

KRISTINA: Ellie, what does 'talent' (**a**) ......*mean*...... ?

ELLIE: Oh, it (**b**) .... something that you are good at.

KRISTINA: OK, I understand. Like I have a talent for singing?

ELLIE: That's right.

KRISTINA: And what do you (**c**) .... it when you like doing something, even if you are not good at it?

ELLIE: You (**d**) .... , like a hobby?

KRISTINA: Yes, a hobby.

ELLIE: Usually people who have hobbies have some kind of ability for the thing they like to do, but not always.

KRISTINA: What do you (**e**) .... by 'ability'?

ELLIE: Ability means being able to do something, like an activity.

KRISTINA: Activity? (**f**) .... that?

ELLIE: An activity is something you do.

KRISTINA: Wow! I need a dictionary. Then I could find these words for myself. How do you (**g**) .... 'find out something for yourself'?

ELLIE: Discover. Yes, I think you need a dictionary, Kristina.

Now listen to Track 13.1 and check your answers.

2 Complete these questions.

a What ....*do*.......... you ......*mean*...... by discipline?

b 'Attention'? What's .... ?

c What .... 'comfortable' .... ?

d How .... 'not calm', running around, acting crazy?

e What .... when something makes you feel afraid?

Now match questions a – e to these answers.

1 Wild.
2 It means you feel at ease, relaxed.
3 It frightens you.
4 It's when you have strict rules.
5 It's when someone talks to you and takes notice of what you do.

a ..*4*..   b ....   c ....   d ....   e ....

3 Complete this dialogue by writing in the correct question from the list below.

> How do you say
> What does that mean
> How do you say this
> What do you call it

ABBY: I really don't like parties.

(**a**) .... when you don't like to meet people?

CHRIS: Shy? Are you shy?

ABBY: Yes, I am. (**b**) .... when something makes you feel afraid?

CHRIS: You mean, it frightens you.

ABBY: Yes, that's right.

CHRIS: That's strange, because you're very popular.

ABBY: Popular? (**c**) .... ?

CHRIS: It's when a lot of people like you.

ABBY: Yes, I think I'm popular, but I don't like it when people take notice of me? (**d**) .... ?

CHRIS: Oh, you mean when people pay you a lot of attention.

ABBY: That's right. I like to stay by myself.

Now listen to Track 13.2 and read Abby's part when it's your turn, after each beep.

Study grammar: *going to*

⟶ see 4A in the Mini-grammar

4 Read the conversation and complete it with the correct form of *going to*.

LAURA: So, what (**a**) *are you going to do* (do) this weekend, Frank?

FRANK: Well, (**b**) .... (go) to a party on Saturday.

LAURA: Great! Whose party?

FRANK: My uncle John (**c**) .... (get) married on Saturday and he and his wife (**d**) .... (have) a big reception in the evening.

LAURA: (**e**) .... (take) anyone with you?

FRANK: No, (**f**) .... (take) anyone.

LAURA: Oh.

FRANK: What (**g**) .... (do) on Saturday?

LAURA: Nothing. (**h**) .... (do) anything.

5 Look at these pictures and write what is going to happen.

a *They are going to have breakfast.*

b ....

c ....

d ....

6 Read these situations. Are the sentences in bold true or false? Correct the sentences that are false.

a It has started to rain and Steve and Lisa don't have an umbrella.
They are not going to get wet.
False. They're going to get wet.

b David studies mathematics every day. He is very good at maths.
He's going to fail the mathematics exam.
....
....

c John and Emma are wearing skis.
They're going to go swimming.
....
....

d There are black clouds everywhere and it's cold.
It's going to rain.
....
....

e Richard and Charlie are sitting at their desks with their English textbooks open.
They're going to play video games.
....
....

f The film starts at 8.30 pm. Julia and Michael live twenty miles from the cinema. They are leaving their house at 8.15 pm.
They are going to be late for the film.
....

Pronunciation: *to*

7 Listen to these sentences on Track 13.3 and underline the syllable that has the main stress.

  a We're going to go to the <u>beach</u>.
  b She's going to win.
  c James is going to study French.
  d They're going to tell you to stop.

Now listen to the pronunciation of *to* in each sentence on Track 13.3. Practise saying the sentences with the same pronunciation of *to*.

8 Write five sentences about yourself using *going to*. Practise your sentences using the appropriate pronunciation of *to*.

Study vocabulary: abilities and talents

9 Put these letters in the right order to make words to describe abilities and talents.

  a tropsy .... *sporty* ....
  b tansingdreund ....
  c carpclati ....
  d blecioas ....
  e nonfidcet ....
  f recavite ....
  g trisacit ....
  h gillaco ....

Now, match the words (a – h) to the definitions (1 – 8).

  1 you are good at working things out step by step
  2 you like meeting people and being with friends
  3 you are good at art, like drawing and painting
  4 you have good original ideas
  5 you are not shy and you are very sure of yourself
  6 you are a good listener and think about other people's feelings
  7 you like playing sports
  8 you can fix things and you don't panic in a crisis

  a ..7.. **b** .... **c** .... **d** .... **e** .... **f** .... **g** .... **h** ....

10 Complete these advertisements with a suitable word or expression.

a

Do you have _green fingers_ **?**

We need someone to help us once a week in our garden. We grow mostly flowers and some vegetables.

Call us on 9384973.

b

We are looking for an .... person to help us draw posters for a concert next month.
Contact: Josie

c

Do you have great ideas? Can you make something out of nothing? Then you might be the .... person we are looking for.

Call John at 6748392

d

I'm looking for a .... person to help me keep my books. I need someone who can go through all my receipts and information and organise it for me.
Mrs Murphy 7849504

e

We need a .... person who loves to meet other people and loves parties. We are professional party organizers.

Write to: Suzie
Contact@greatparties.com

f

Are you .... ?
Do you love to play games? Come and try out for our new basketball team.
We need you!
Come to the gym on Friday at 2 pm.

11 Word Bank

Write the names of ten people you know and use the new words from this unit to describe them in your Word Bank notebook.

Example: My dad: sporty, practical, sociable

Study grammar: *will* and *going to*

➡ see 4A, 4B and 4C in the Mini-grammar

12 Underline the best answer to complete these conversations.

a MANDY: What are you going to study?
JEFF: *I will study* / *I'm going to study* law.

b MUM: What are you going to do tomorrow?
MELISSA: I'm not sure yet. *I'll probably stay* / *I'm going to stay* at home.

c OLD MAN: Oh, these books are heavy.
YOUNG WOMAN: Do you need help? *I'll carry* / *I'm going to carry* your books for you.
OLD MAN: Thanks, dear.

d MARTHA: *What are you going to do* / *What will you do* in the holidays?
PETE: *We're going to go* / *We will go* to Spain.
MARTHA: That's nice.

e MIKE: I don't know what to write. I have to write a letter.
LISA: I have an idea. Give me that pen – *I'll write* / *I'm going to write* the letter for you.
MIKE: Thanks.

f DARREN: Right. Here's my plan. I'm not going to paint the house. *I'm going to get some painters to do it.* / *I'll paint the house.*
LOUISE: That sounds great. *I'll help you look* / *I'm going to help you look*, if you like.
DARREN: That would be great.

13 Match responses 1 – 8 to the questions a – h.

a What are you going to do next weekend? [5]

b Who do you think will win the chess competition? [ ]

c Will you help me with my homework tonight? [ ]

d Do you know what she's going to study? [ ]

e What's he going to be when he grows up? [ ]

f Can you help me with this maths problem? [ ]

g Who will be the next world soccer champion? [ ]

h Are you going to go to Dave's party? [ ]

1 Yes. I'll see you there.
2 Sorry, I can't. I'm going to go to the cinema with Charlie later.
3 I think Jane will beat Mike.
4 Sure. I'll read the problem and you tell me what you don't understand.
5 We're going to visit my grandmother.
6 It's going to be a tough competition, but I think Brazil will win.
7 He's going to be a firefighter.
8 Yes. She's going to study psychology.

How did you do?

14 Can you translate these sentences into your language?

a Children need discipline.

....

b What does the English word 'criminology' mean?

....

c How do you say the English word 'grumpy'?

....

d I'm going to stay at home tonight.

....

e She's going to study law.

....

f What are you going to do when you grow up?

....

g My mother loves gardening. She has green fingers.

....

h Are you an understanding person?

....

15 Evaluation of Just learning in Unit 13

Answer these questions about the Just learning section in Unit 13 page 103 of the Student's Book.

Using language to 'buy time'

When would you *use language to 'buy time'*? Tick the boxes below.

■ when you don't know what to say

■ when you understand everything

■ when there is a word you don't understand

■ when you are confused about something

Write one example of your own.

....

....

How easy is *using language to 'buy time'* for you?

Very easy				Difficult
5	4	3	2	1

Go back and read the Just learning section in the Student's Book. How useful is the advice on *using language to 'buy time'* to you in your language learning?

Very useful				Not useful
5	4	3	2	1

16 Phonetics

Look at the phonemic symbols on page 96. Write these sentences from Unit 13 in normal spelling.

a /ʃiːz gaʊɪŋ wɪən/

   she's going to win.   .

b /aɪm gaʊɪŋ tə gaʊ tə 'pærɪs/

....

c /ɑː juː gaʊɪŋ tə gaʊ tə ðə pɑːtiː/

....

.... ?

d /ɪz hiː gaʊɪŋ pleɪ/

.... ?

Listen to Track 13.4 to check? your answers and then read the words aloud.

UNIT 14 Describing things

Study grammar: *a*, *an* and *the*

⟹ see 2A – 2C in the Mini-grammar

1 Read sentences a – i and match the use of the article *a*, *an* or *the* with reasons 1 – 6 for using it.

a I want to buy **a** new car. ....**1**....

b My brother is **an** artist. ....

c Don't stay in **the** sun too long! ....

d Which kitten do you want? **The** black one or **the** grey one? ....

e Have you been to **the** United Kingdom? ....

f The first man walked on **the** moon in 1969. ....

g I need **a** hammer. Can you pass me **the** hammer, please? ....

h That's **a** good idea! ....

i He's going to **the** USA next week. ....

1 use *a* to talk about one of something
2 use *an* to talk about one of something that begins with a vowel
3 use *the* to talk about one special thing that everybody knows
4 use *the* to talk about something for the second time
5 use *the* to talk about something when people know which one you are talking about
6 use *the* before the name of some countries

2 Say why *no article* is used in each one of the examples 1 – 6.

a zero article before a plural noun describing things in general
b zero article before singular uncountable nouns describing things in general
c zero article before most names of countries

1 I've never eaten snails. ....**a**....

2 She lived in France for ten years. ....

3 Do you like rice? ....

4 When did she move to Kenya? ....

5 No, I don't like cats. ....

6 I never drink coffee in the evening. ....

3 Complete these paragraphs with *a*, *an*, *the*, or *zero article*.

(a) ....**The**.. Eiffel Tower in Paris was built between 1887 and 1889. (b) .... architect was Stephen Sauvestre.

There is (c) .... restaurant on the second level called (d) .... Jules Verne Restaurant and there is (e) .... restaurant on the first level called (f) .... Altitude 95. There are (g) .... shops on the third level and of course there is (h) .... great view of (i) .... city. There are 1,665 steps to (j) .... top of (k) .... tower, but there is also (l) .... elevator.

4 Unjumble these words to find adjectives that describe size.

a raleg   *large* ....

b sonoreum   ....

c nimetu   ....

d ytni   ....

e ibg   ....

f tangicig   ....

g lamsl   ....

h guhe   ....

5 Now put the words in order of size from a–h.

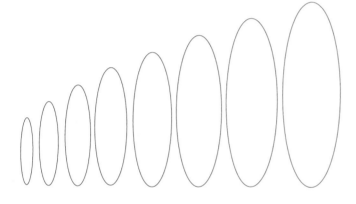

a   *minute*   b ....   c ....

d ....   e ....   f ....

g ....   h ....

6 Now use the words to describe these things:

a your car

....

b your family

....

c the Eiffel Tower

....

d where you live

....

7 Look at the pictures and complete the sentences with one of these words.

long ◆ wide ◆ high ◆ tall ◆ deep ◆ shallow

a The water is ...... *shallow* ....

b The road is very ....

c This tree is very ....

d The road is not very ....

e This hole is very ....

f The woman is very ....

8 Word Bank

In your Word Bank notebook write one thing you know that is:

minute ◆ tiny ◆ small ◆ big ◆ large ◆ huge ◆ enormous ◆ gigantic ◆ long ◆ wide ◆ high ◆ tall deep ◆ shallow

Example: Minute – Her writing is minute. I can't read it.

Study grammar: superlative adjectives

➡ see 1C in the Mini-grammar

9 Complete these sentences using the superlative form of the adjective in brackets.

a This is ...*the worst*... (bad) film I have ever seen!

b *A Brief History of Time* is .... (interesting) book I have ever read.

c Would you like to live in .... (large) city in the world?

d I think this is .... (uncomfortable) chair I have ever sat in.

e They went to .... (cheap) restaurant in the city, because they had very little money.

f The Lamborghini Murciélago is one of .... (expensive) cars in the world.

g Charlie Chaplin's films are still some of .... (funny) movies ever.

h What do you think is .... (good) way to get to the bridge from here?

i Try to cross the river here, because this is .... (narrow) part.

j Richie is .... (thin) of my three nephews.

10 Complete these questions. Then find the answers.

a Which is ...*the tallest*... (tall) building in the world?
   Taipei 101 Tower in Taipei, Taiwan (1,670 ft or 509 m).

b What is .... (long) river in Europe?
   ....
   ....

c Who is .... (tall) person in the world?
   ....
   ....

d What is .... (high) mountain in South America?
   ....
   ....

Study functions: comparing experiences

11 Put these words in order to make sentences. Use capital letters where necessary. In a different order, the sentences make a conversation.

a your / take / time / . /
   Take your time.

b sounds / that / nice / . /
   ....

c made / chicken / with / she / gravy / and / roast / roast / potatoes / . /
   ....
   ....

d have / I'll / think / to / . /
   ....

e loved / yes, / it / everyone / . /
   ....

f the / eaten / what's / delicious / ever / was / you've / most / meal / ? /
   ....
   ....

g she / did / cook / what / ? /
   ....

h birthday / eighteenth / mum / the / it / for / my / was / meal / cooked / my /. /
   ....
   ....
   ....

12 Now put the sentences in order to make the short conversation.
   f ....

🔊 Listen to Track 14.1 to check your answers.

13 Now answer these questions about yourself.

   What was the most delicious meal you've ever eaten?
   ....
   ....

   Who cooked it?
   ....

   What did that person (or people) cook?
   ....
   ....

🔊 Now listen to Track 14.2 and speak when it's your turn.

14 Look at these words and think about how you say them. Put them into the correct column.

beautiful ◆ ugly ◆ delicious ◆ horrible ◆ enjoyable ◆ boring ◆
frightening ◆ bad ◆ cheap ◆ cramped ◆ deep ◆ expensive ◆ fast ◆
fat ◆ funny ◆ good ◆ high ◆ interesting ◆ long ◆ narrow ◆
spacious ◆ thin ◆ uncomfortable

One syllable	Two syllables	Three syllables	Four syllables
cramped	spacious	beautiful	

Now listen to Track 14.3 and check your answers.

15 Now listen to Track 14.4 and draw the stress pattern for the words you hear.

a beautiful ▢▫▫..........

b delicious ....

c boring ....

d enjoyable ....

e frightening ....

f funny ....

g expensive ....

h interesting ....

i spacious ....

j narrow ....

k uncomfortable ....

How did you do?

16 Find the mistake and write the correct version.

wrong	right
a It looks like modern building.	It looks like a modern building.
b That person looks like happy.	
c I love the chocolate. It's my favourite food.	
d Do you need chair?	
e We're going to visit United States.	
f Look at that mountain. It's very tall.	
g My watch is very small. It's gigantic.	
h That was the funnyest movie I've ever seen.	
i He's the most fat person in the world.	
j This is the interestingest book I've read.	

17 Evaluation of the Just learning in Unit 14

Answer these questions about the Just learning section in Unit 14 page 113 of the Student's Book.

Using a dictionary

When would you *use a dictionary*? Tick the boxes below.

- ▨ to look up words you don't know
- ▨ to find out how words are pronounced
- ▨ to help you to have a conversation with someone
- ▨ to learn new words

Write one example of your own.

....

....

How easy is *using a dictionary* for you?

Very easy				Difficult
5	4	3	2	1

Go back and read the Just learning section in the Student's Book. How useful is the advice about *using a dictionary* to you in your language learning?

Very useful				Not useful
5	4	3	2	1

18 Phonetics

Look at the phonemic symbols on page 96. Write these words from Unit 14 in normal spelling.

a /drə'mætɪk/ dramatic

b /'mɒdən/ ....

c /'ʌgli/ ....

d /'diːvə/ ....

e /maɪ'njuːt/ ....

f /ɪ'nɔːməs/ ....

g /'ʃæləʊ/ ....

h /waɪd/ ....

i /wɜːst/ ....

j /'ʃɔːtɪst/ ....

Listen to Track 14.5 to check your answers and then read the words aloud.

A healthy mind and a healthy body

Study vocabulary: The head and face

1 Look at these pictures. Can you identify the parts of the head and face? Write the word.

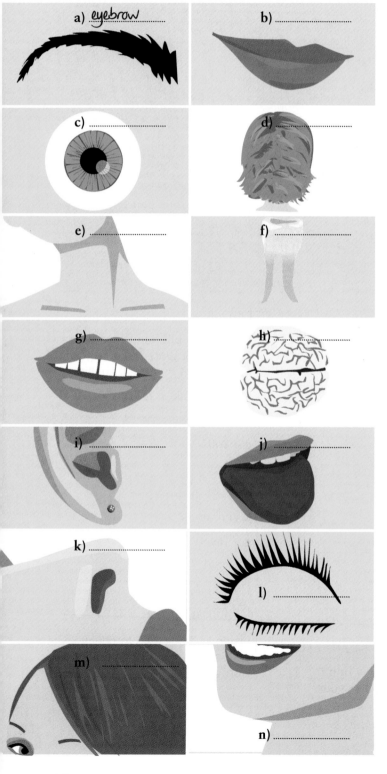

a) eyebrow

b) ....

c) ....

d) ....

e) ....

f) ....

g) ....

h) ....

i) ....

j) ....

k) ....

l) ....

m) ....

n) ....

2 Use one of the words from Exercise 1 to complete these sentences.

a You need your ....teeth.......... to bite something.

b People often wear earrings in their

....

c Your .... protect your eyes.

d The holes in your nose are called

....

e Your .... is at the bottom of your face.

f We use our .... to kiss.

g It's very long – I need to cut my ....

h The top of your face is called your

....

i Your .... are above your eyes.

j If you wear contact lenses, you wear them on

your ....

k You need your .... to speak and to taste.

l Your head rests on top of your ....

m You need your .... to think.

3 Word Bank

In your Word Bank notebook draw a picture of the head and face and label all the parts that you know. Now write all the verbs you know that use parts of the head and face next to the parts you use.

Mouth: talk, eat, smile, etc...

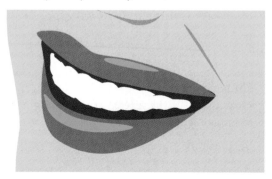

Study grammar: first conditional

→ see 3B in the Mini-grammar

4 Read these sentences from advertisements and complete them with the correct verb tenses.

a If you .... *like* .... (like) chocolate, you ....*will love*.... (love) our new chocolate chew bar.

b You .... (have) whiter teeth if you .... (use) our new toothpaste.

c Your clothes .... (stay) cleaner longer if you .... (wash) them with Brite washing powder.

d If your child .... (be) over three years old, she or he .... (enjoy) playing with the Shape Game.

e You .... (not be) sorry if you .... (change) to the Best Bank.

f If you .... (not have) time to eat, our new soup .... (fill) you up and .... (save) you time.

5 Now match each sentence from Exercise 4 to the correct picture.

1 ___

2 ___

3 ___

4 ___

5 ___

6 ___

6 Write sentences for these advertisements using the first conditional.

a

....

....

b

....

....

c

....

....

d

....

....

7 Complete this conversation with one of the phrases below.

> Neither can I. ◆ I do, too. ◆ Me too! ◆
> I'm not either. ◆ So do I. ◆ Neither do I.

RICHARD: I need to wear glasses.

ALICE: (**a**) _So do I_. I can't read the newspaper very well.

RICHARD: (**b**) .... It gives me a headache.

ALICE: (**c**) .... But I don't know any good opticians.

RICHARD: (**d**) ...., but my sister knows one.

ALICE: That's good. Can you give me the name when you've asked her?

RICHARD: Sure. I need to have my eyes tested soon.

ALICE: (**e**) .... Call me tonight, I'm not going out.

RICHARD: (**f**) .... I'll call you around seven.

ALICE: OK. Thanks.

Now listen to Track 15.1 and check your answers.

8 Look at this information about Maria and Claire and write appropriate sentences about their similarities and differences.

> Name: Maria Smith
> Age: 22
> Occupation: Psychology student
> Marital status: Single
> Hometown: London
> Address: 15 High St, Wimbledon

> Name: Claire Smith
> Age: 22
> Occupation: Medical student
> Marital status: Single
> Hometown: London
> Address: 26 Merton Court, Wimbledon

a Maria's last name is Smith.
   So is Claire's.

b Claire is from London.

....

c Maria is a student.

....

d Claire is studying medicine.

....

e Claire isn't married.

....

f Maria lives in Wimbledon.

....

9 Now complete this dialogue between Maria and Claire.

MARIA: Hi, my name's Maria Smith.

CLAIRE: My name's Smith, (**a**) _too_ .

MARIA: Oh really? Where are you from?

CLAIRE: I'm from London.

MARIA: (**b**) .... ! Where do you live?

CLAIRE: In Wimbledon.

MARIA: (**c**) .... Are you married?

CLAIRE: No, I'm (**d**)

....

MARIA: (**e**) .... I. What do you do?

CLAIRE: I'm a student.

MARIA: (**f**) .... What are you studying?

CLAIRE: Medicine. Are you studying medicine,

(**g**) .... ?

MARIA: No, (**h**) .... I'm studying psychology.

Listen to Track 15.2 and speak as Claire.

10 Listen to Track 15.3 and say whether the pronunciation of the underlined word is the same (S) or different (D).

garage

a He put the car in the garage.
He put the car in the garage.

.....*S*.....

b The paint is in the garage.
The paint is in the garage.

....

room

c John is upstairs in his room.
John is upstairs in his room.

....

d What do you think of this room?
What do you think of this room?

....

new

e I really need some new shoes.
I really need some new shoes.

....

f This DVD is new.
This DVD is new.

....

11 Now listen to Track 15.3 again and circle the phonetic transcription that you hear.

   a /gəˈrɑːʒ/   /ˈgærɪdʒ/
       /gəˈrɑːʒ/   /ˈgærɪdʒ/
   b /gəˈrɑːʒ/   /ˈgærɪdʒ/
       /gəˈrɑːʒ/   /ˈgærɪdʒ/
   c /ruːm/   /rʊm/
       /ruːm/   /rʊm/
   d /ruːm/   /rʊm/
       /ruːm/   /rʊm/
   e /nuː/   /njuː/
       /nuː/   /njuː/
   f /nuː/   /njuː/
       /nuː/   /njuː/

Practise saying the sentences with the same pronunciation as Track 15.3.

⟹ see 3A and 3B in the Mini-grammar

12 Read this article and choose the best way to complete these sentences.

   a You will damage your hair
   1 <u>if you don't eat enough iron.</u>
   2 if you eat vegetables.

   b If you eat plenty of vitamin C,
   1 your hair won't be healthy.
   2 your hair will shine.

   c If you cut your hair regularly,
   1 it will be easier to take care of.
   2 it will become stronger.

   d If you use hair products,
   1 they never damage your hair.
   2 you must be careful.

Healthy Hair

Here are some tips for men and women to keep your hair healthy.

First, you need to have enough iron in your diet. If not, you will damage your hair. Your hair stays healthy when you eat foods like meat, eggs, cereals and vegetables like spinach.

Secondly, to make your hair healthy and shiny, you must eat fruits and vegetables that contain vitamin C.

Thirdly, it is a good idea to cut your hair regularly. It does not become thicker or stronger when it is cut, but cutting your hair makes it easier to take care of.

Finally, be careful with the products that you use on your hair. When you colour your hair you can damage it. Some people have more delicate hair, so you should test a new product before you use it to see what happens to your hair.

If your hair is hurt by a product or if your scalp is allergic to a hair product, you must stop using that product to stop the problem from getting worse.

13 Complete these sentences with information from the text:

   a If you don't eat enough vitamin C, ...
   b It is easier to take care of your hair if ....
   c If you colour your hair, ...
   d If you have delicate hair, ...

14 Look at the sentences in Exercises 12 and 13 and write zero (for zero conditional) or first (for first conditional).

   12 a ...*first*...   b ....   c ....   d ....

   13 a ....   b ....   c ....   d ....

How did you do?

15 Can you translate these sentences into your language?

a If you don't lie down, you won't be able to sleep.

....

b You'll catch a cold if you go out in the rain.

....

c If you want to stay healthy, you have to eat well.

....

d A: I've just started a new school. B: Me too.

....

e A: I'm very tired. B: So am I.

....

f A: I don't do much exercise. B: Neither do I.

....

g A: He doesn't like swimming. B: I don't, either.

....

h I always get tired if I run more than five miles.

....

16 Evaluation of Just learning in Unit 15

Answer these questions about the Just learning section in Unit 15 page 120 of the Student's Book.

Working out the rule for yourself

When would you *work out the rule for yourself*? Tick the boxes below.

☐ to help you to understand a grammar rule

☐ to help you to listen more carefully

☐ to understand a word you don't know

☐ to use a grammar book

Write one example of your own.

....

....

How easy is *working out the rule for yourself* for you?

Very easy   Difficult

   5   4   3   2   1

Go back and read the Just learning section in the Student's Book. How useful is the advice about *working out the rule for yourself* to you in your language learning?

Very useful   Not useful

   5   4   3   2   1

17 Phonetics

Look at the phonemic symbols on page 96. Write these words from Unit 15 in normal spelling.

a /ˈaɪðə/ /ˈiːðə/   *either*

b /ˈniːðə/ /ˈnaɪðə/ ....

c /rʊm/ /ruːm/   ....

d /ˈgærɪdʒ/
/gəˈrɑːʒ/   ....

e /nuː/ /njuː/   ....

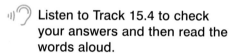 Listen to Track 15.4 to check your answers and then read the words aloud.

UNIT 16 Weird and wonderful

Study vocabulary: from strange to amazing

1 Find twelve adjectives in this word search. Look down, up, diagonally and side to side.

```
W O N D E R F U L  D O O
E D I E W R F U L U N B
I D S T R A A G N A M A
R S C A R E M Z A N U N
D C I T S A T N A F Y N
S R O G O P O J H G F L
T E E N R U N U S U L A
R E P I N E A P P L E U
A P A Z A M A Y R A C S
N Y F A U N N T D O D U
G E A M I E V A B L E N
E L B A V E I L E B N U
```

2 Write suitable words about the pictures to describe them.

a b

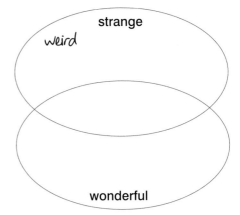

c

d

4 Word Bank

Make a diagram like this in your Word Bank notebook with all the words you know for things that are strange, wonderful or both.

strange

weird

wonderful

3 Write a description of one of the pictures using at least five adjectives.

....

....

....

....

Study grammar: review of present, past and future tenses

➡ see 4, 8 and 10 in the Mini-grammar

5 Read these sentences and write whether they refer to the past, the present or the future.

a This house was built in 1965. (passive) ....._past_.....

b Next week we're visiting my grandmother in France. ....

c I'm working on a grammar exercise at the moment. ....

d My mother has lived in Russia for twenty years. ....

e My car is being washed at the moment. (passive) ....

f Did you watch that TV programme last night? ....

g Will you help me with my homework tonight? ....

h We live by the sea. ....

i Last night at nine o'clock I was watching TV. ....

6 Name the tense used in each sentence in Exercise 5.

a _past simple (passive)_ ....

b ....

c ....

d ....

e ....

f ....

g ....

h ....

i ....

7 Complete these dialogues with the correct tense.

A

JAMES: Where (a) _does_ he _live_ (live) now?

MARIE: He (b) .... (live) in a strange little house in the mountains.

B

MARTIN: (a) .... you ever .... (be) to Egypt?

JOANNE: No, I (b) .... , but I'm (c) .... (go) to Cairo next year.

C

MUM: What time (a) .... your train .... (leave) yesterday?

BOBBY: It (b) .... (leave) at 9 and (c) .... (arrive) at 11.30.

D

OLD MAN: I can't open this door. (a) .... you .... (help) me?

YOUNG WOMAN: Of course! I (b) .... (open) it for you.

8 Complete this paragraph with an appropriate verb form for each gap.

In the future ...

Stephen Hawking, the world famous physicist, (a) _has been_ (be) worried for a long time about computers. He (b) .... (be) worried because computers (c) .... (develop) very quickly. He (d) .... (think) that, in the future, computers (e) .... (become) more intelligent than humans. He (f) .... (believe) that computers with artificial intelligence could control the world.

Study functions: paying attention

9 Complete this dialogue with expressions from the box. You will not need them all and you may want to use some of them more than once.

> Yeah? ◆ What happened next? ◆ Really? ◆
> Uh-huh ◆ Then what happened? ◆
> What did she say? ◆ What? ◆ How weird! ◆
> That's funny. ◆ Right. ◆ That's impossible! ◆
> Wow! ◆ And? ◆ That's weird. ◆ That's strange. ◆
> I see.

JANE: So, let me tell you about what happened at the airport.

ROBBIE: (**a**) _Uh–huh._

JANE: Well, I arrived early to check in.

ROBBIE: (**b**) ....

JANE: And then I went to get something to eat.

ROBBIE: (**c**) ....

JANE: While I was eating a sandwich I heard someone scream.

ROBBIE: (**d**) ....

JANE: Well, I ran to where I heard the scream.

ROBBIE: (**e**) ....

JANE: And, you'll never guess what?

ROBBIE: (**f**) ....

JANE: There was nobody there.

ROBBIE: (**g**) ....

JANE: Well, I looked and looked everywhere for the person in trouble.

ROBBIE: (**h**) ....

JANE: I never found anything. And do you know what was the worst thing?

ROBBIE: (**i**) ....

JANE: I missed the plane, because I was looking for the person who screamed.

ROBBIE: (**j**) ....

Now listen to Track 16.1 and compare your answers.

10 Listen to the story on Track 16.2 and reply as Robbie.

Pronunciation: spelling words

11 Listen to the words being spelled on Track 16.3 and write them down.

a ....
....

b ....
....

c ....
....

d ....
....

Now write the acronyms for the phrases you have written above.

a ....

b ....

c ....

d ....

Practise spelling the words out loud.

Study grammar: review of adjectives and prepositions, articles and quantifiers

⇒see 1, 2, 6 and 9 in the Mini-grammar

12 Read the text and look at the words a – i below. Circle the best choice for each gap in the text and fill it in.

Two women were walking **a)** ~through~ a local cemetery filming with a video camera. Suddenly **b)** .... camera stopped working. They kept taping with **c)** .... portable tape recorder that one woman had **d)** .... her pocket. They chatted about the beauty of the cemetery as they walked **e)** .... the path.

Later when they listened to **f)** .... recording, they heard something very strange. After one of **g)** .... women said "What **h)** .... peaceful area," a creepy whisper said "peaceful." They played **i)** .... tape about 20 times and heard the voice each time.

a	1) over	2) below	3) (through)
b	1) one	2) the	3) a
c	1) a	2) the	3) an
d	1) in	2) to	3) of
e	1) into	2) along	3) inside
f	1) ----	2) a	3) the
g	1) the	2) a	3) one
h	1) one	2) a	3) ----
i	1) a	2) the	3) ----

◁) Now listen to Track 16.4 to check your answers.

How did you do?

13 Find the mistake and write the correct version.

wrong	right
a I love this car. It's creepy.	I love this car. It's fantastic.
b The people is built a city in the desert.	
c We used go to the movies when I was a child.	
d The sun was shine when I got out of bed.	
e Have you hear this CD yet?	
f That impossible!	
g I don't want some sugar.	
h Put those apples in the table.	
i How much UFOs have you seen?	
j My car has being washed.	

14 Evaluation of the Just learning in Unit 16

Answer these questions about the Just learning section in Unit 16 page 131 of the Student's Book.

Telling stories again

How can *telling stories again* help you? Tick the boxes below.

- ▨ to help you to remember words and grammar
- ▨ to help you to read more quickly
- ▨ to write better stories
- ▨ to improve your pronunciation

Write one idea of your own.

....

....

....

....

How easy is *telling stories again* for you?

Very easy   Difficult

5   4   3   2   1

Go back and read the Just learning section in the Student's Book. How useful is the advice about *telling stories again* in your language learning?

Very useful   Not useful

5   4   3   2   1

15 Phonetics

Look at the phonemic symbols on page 96. Write these words from Unit 16 in normal spelling.

a /wiːəd/   weird

b /ˈskeəriː/ ....

c /əˈmeɪzɪŋ/ ....

d /spekˈteɪtəz/ ....

e /ˈsʌnblɒk/   ....

f /waʊ/   ....

g /ˈjuːˈefˈəʊ/ ....

h /ˈbiːˈbiːˈsiː/ ....

◁))) Listen to track 16.5 to check your answers and then read the words aloud.

Audioscript

TRACK 1.1

SAM: Which package is better, then?

JACK: Oh, Package 3, definitely. It's cheaper! Which do you prefer?

SAM: Me? I prefer Package 1. It sounds much nicer.

JACK: But it's more expensive and shorter. Anyway, I prefer summer holidays to winter holidays.

SAM: But the summer is nice here, too. I'd rather go in December, when it's dark and cold here.

JACK: OK, you win. But that's the only holiday we can take in the whole year then. Would you rather have just one holiday or two? Think about it.

SAM: Oh. Maybe July is not so bad after all...

Track 1.2

BEEP

JACK: Oh, Package 3, definitely. It's cheaper! Which do you prefer?

BEEP

JACK: But it's more expensive and shorter. Anyway, I prefer summer holidays to winter holidays.

BEEP

JACK: OK, you win. But that's the only holiday we can take in the whole year then. Would you rather have just one holiday or two? Think about it.

Track 1.3

a phone box
b letter box
c tea cup
d road signs
e park bench
f traffic lights
g cricket match
h underground station

Track 1.4

a Australia
b New Zealand
c Great Britain
d Ireland
e Jamaica
f Scotland
g The USA

Track 2.1

ROB: Hi Leyla! You don't look too happy. Problems?

LEYLA: I have exams next week and I don't know anything! What can I do to pass?

ROB: Hey, relax! Try studying your notes.

LEYLA: Yeah, I looked at them but it doesn't help.

ROB: Well, of course, just looking doesn't help. You can do some of the practice questions, too.

LEYLA: Hmm, yes. But what about maths? I don't understand anything! Got any ideas?

ROB: Well, you could do some of the exercises in the book. Don't worry! That's my advice!

LEYLA: You're right. Let's forget about exams. Do you want to listen to my new JLo record?

Track 2.2

ROB: Hi Leyla! You don't look too happy. Problems?

LEYLA: I have exams next week and I don't know anything! What can I do to pass?

BEEP

LEYLA: Yeah, I looked at them but it doesn't help.

BEEP

LEYLA: Hmm, yes. But what about maths? I don't understand anything! Got any ideas?

BEEP

LEYLA: You're right. Let's forget about exams. Do you want to listen to my new JLo record?

Track 2.3

a problem
b result

Track 2.4

c coffee
d chocolate
e water
f inside
g salad
h without
i practise

Track 2.5

a chocolate
b coffee
c much
d few
e advice
f many

Track 3.1

LOUISE: What do you think of documentaries?

DAMIAN: I think they're boring.

LOUISE: Do you really think so?

DAMIAN: Yes, don't you?

LOUISE: No. I think they're interesting. Well, sometimes.

DAMIAN: I think you're right. Only sometimes. I hate documentaries about animals, for example.

LOUISE: Oops! I bought you a DVD about birds for your birthday.
DAMIAN: You're joking!
LOUISE: No. I really did.
DAMIAN: Oh, well, birds are fine. Birds are good. Actually, I love birds!

Track 3.2
BEEP
DAMIAN: I think they're boring.
BEEP
DAMIAN: Yes, don't you?
BEEP
DAMIAN: I think you're right. Only sometimes. I hate documentaries about animals, for example.
BEEP
DAMIAN: You're joking!
BEEP
DAMIAN: Oh, well, birds are fine. Birds are good. Actually, I love birds!

Track 3.3
ANNOUNCER: These words have the sound /ʃ/:
WOMAN: sugar
solution
fashion
discussion
ANNOUNCER: These words have the sound /ʒ/:
WOMAN: usually
conclusion
television
decision

Track 3.4
a How do you like your tea?
BEEP
b Come on then. What's the solution?
BEEP
c What are you doing?
BEEP
d So, what do you think?
BEEP

Track 3.5
a watch
b what
c radio
d usual
e agree
f media

Track 4.1
MAN: Are you looking for a job?
WOMAN: Are you interested in people?
MAN: Are you good with animals?
WOMAN: Can you work in a team?
MAN: Do you like working with animals?

Track 4.2
MAN: Are you looking for a job? How would you like to help animals? Can you work in a team? Yes? We've got the perfect job for you. Call the Animal Hospital now! No experience required!

Track 4.3
MAX: I am thinking of teaching after college. But I'm not sure.
MOLLY: Teaching? You? But you don't like children.
MAX: I'm not very keen on them. But I don't hate them. Actually, I don't really mind children – for a short time!
MOLLY: I love little children but I can't stand big groups. I fancy a job teaching small groups.
MAX: Oh no, that's not for me. I want to get a temporary job to see if I like it.
MOLLY: That's a good idea.

Track 4.4
INTERVIEWER: How do you feel about children?
BEEP
INTERVIEWER: Right. Now, tell me two things you like about teaching.
BEEP
INTERVIEWER: And two things you definitely don't like?
BEEP
INTERVIEWER: So, do you think teaching is right for you?
BEEP

Track 4.5
a job
b checking
c work
d playing
e does
f love

Track 5.1
JACKIE: Where's the best place to meet?
SANDY: Where do you suggest?
JACKIE: Why don't we meet at Café Commons?
SANDY: OK. What time?
JACKIE: Hmm. How about 7.30?
SANDY: That sounds great.
JACKIE: OK. 7.30 it is, then.
SANDY: See you there.

Track 5.2

BEEP

MAYA: Let's say 6 o'clock.

BEEP

MAYA: We could meet at the bus stop.

BEEP

MAYA: OK. Good idea. We'll meet at the restaurant.

BEEP

MAYA: See you there.

Track 5.3

a check

b train

c plane

d left

e get

f bay

g take

h say

i then

j better

k gate

Track 5.4

a station

b ferry

c bus

d train

e plane

f escalator

Track 6.1

a What's your name?

b When were you born?

c Are you married?

d Are your grandparents still living?

e Are you keen on anyone in particular?

f At what age did you start school?

Track 6.2

a How nice!

b How awful!

c How funny!

d How boring!

e How exciting!

Track 6.3

a I have to work on Saturday.

BEEP

b My grandfather fell and broke his leg.

BEEP

c I'm going to Australia!

BEEP

d Ryan got married in a Superman suit!

BEEP

e Look, I bought you an ice cream.

BEEP

Track 6.4

ALEX: I did something really stupid.

BERNIE: Let me guess! You lost your mobile phone again, right?

ALEX: No, no. I'm seeing Paula tonight, right? So I bought her some flowers.

BERNIE: That's nice.

ALEX: Yeah. But I put the flowers on the roof of the car, you know, to open the door.

BERNIE: Uh, oh.

ALEX: And I drove away with the flowers on the roof. Now I feel really stupid.

BERNIE: I know the feeling. So, buy her more flowers.

ALEX: I don't have money for the cinema and more flowers.

BERNIE: That sounds familiar!

Track 6.5

ALEX: I did something really stupid.

BEEP

ALEX: No, no. I'm seeing Paula tonight, right? So I bought her some flowers.

BEEP

ALEX: Yeah. But I put the flowers on the roof of the car, you know, to open the door.

BEEP

ALEX: And I drove away with the flowers on the roof. Now I feel really stupid.

BEEP

ALEX: I don't have money for the cinema and more flowers.

BEEP

Track 6.6

GIRL 1: I did something really stupid.

GIRL 2: Let me guess! You lost your glasses again.

GIRL 1: No. I bought a cake for my sister's birthday.

GIRL 2: That's kind.

GIRL 1: But I put it on my chair and I sat on it!

GIRL 2: How stupid! Buy her another cake.

GIRL 1: I haven't got any more money!

GIRL 2: I know the feeling!

Track 6.7

a memory

b married

c birth

d death

e lovely

f used to

g remember

Track 7.1

1 bingo

2 swimming

3 no

4 sound

5 drink

6 fun

7 sun

8 sung

9 thanks

10 thin

11 thing

12 think

Track 7.2

MAN: Listen to these words with the sound /n/.

WOMAN: no   sound   fun   sun   thin

MAN: Now, listen to these words with the sound /ŋ/.

WOMAN: bingo   swimming   drink   sung   thanks
thing   think

Track 7.3

JAMIE: Hey, Nat. Would you like to come bowling?

NAT: Bowling? I'd love to, Jamie, but I can't. I have to work.

JAMIE: Oh, well. Perhaps another day?

NAT: Yeah. Perhaps.

SUE: Hi, Sam. Do you fancy going to the cinema?

SAM: Hmm. I'm not sure, Sue. I went to the cinema on
Saturday.

SUE: How about a pizza then?

SAM: That would be great. I'm really hungry.

TRICIA: Would you like to come to dinner tonight, Mike?

MIKE: I'd rather not, Tricia. I have to get up early tomorrow.

TRICIA: How about Friday then?

MIKE: I'm not really sure. Call me tomorrow, OK?

TRICIA: OK.

Track 7.4

BEEP

MIKE: A dance? Well, I don't really like dancing.

BEEP

MIKE: I'd love to but I'm busy on Tuesday.

BEEP

MIKE: Now you're talking! Everybody says you're a
great cook!

Track 7.5

a bowling

b leisure

c inviting

d like-minded

e ironing

f listening

g confident

h creativity

Track 8.1

a

MAN: Was the test difficult?

GIRL: No. It was nice and easy.

b

WOMAN: Can you come and help?

MAN: Yes, I can. But I can only stay for an hour.

c

WOMAN: How was your holiday?

MAN: Jamaica was hot and humid!

WOMAN: But was it nice?

MAN: Oh, it was beautiful – and a lot of fun!

Track 8.2

a Was the test difficult?

BEEP

b Can you come and help?

BEEP

c How was your holiday?

BEEP

d But was it nice?

BEEP

Track 8.3

a

MAN: You're late!

WOMAN: Sorry!

MAN: Well, we said 8 o'clock and it's 8.45 now.

WOMAN: I know. I'm sorry you waited so long.

MAN: It wasn't much fun, you know?

WOMAN: I said I'm sorry. I lost my laptop. That's why
I'm late.

MAN: Oh, I'm really sorry. I didn't mean to upset you.
Listen, do you still want to see the film?

b

WOMAN: Good afternoon, Mr Rice. I apologise for being late.

MAN: Yes, I see your appointment was at four.

WOMAN: I'm sorry. There was a lot of traffic.

MAN: Well, never mind. Now, open wide please.

WOMAN: Ouch!

MAN: Oops, sorry. Did that hurt?

Track 8.4

MAN: You're late!

BEEP

MAN: Well, we said 8 o'clock and it's 8.45 now.

BEEP

MAN: It wasn't much fun, you know?

BEEP

MAN: Oh, I'm really sorry. I didn't mean to upset you. Listen,
do you still want to see the film?

Track 8.5

a apologise

b sorry

c smiling

d everybody

e jealous

f worry

Track 9.1

MAN 1: Hello? Eton Electronics.
MAN 2: Can I speak to Larry, please?
MAN 1: He's not in today. Can I take a message?
MAN 2: No thanks. That's OK.

ANSWERING MACHINE: Hi! This is Lisa. I can't take your call at the moment. Please leave a message after the tone.

RECEPTIONIST: This is the Richmond Clinic. How can I help you?
MAN 2: Can you put me through to Dr Lewis?
RECEPTIONIST: Her line's busy. Would you like to hold?
MAN 2: No thanks. I'll call later.

WOMAN: Hello.
MAN 2: Hi. Is Jane there please?
WOMAN: This is Jane.
MAN 2: Oh, Jane. Great! How are you?
WOMAN: Ricky? What a surprise! What can I do for you?
MAN 2: Nothing really. I just wanted to talk to somebody and nobody else is in!

Track 9.2

BEEP
FRANCES: Hi. This is Frances. Can I speak to Carmen, please?
BEEP
FRANCES: When will she be back?
BEEP
FRANCES: Yes, please. Tell her Frances called. Can she meet me outside the cinema at 8.30, not at 8. I can't be there earlier.
BEEP
FRANCES: That's right. Who's speaking please?
BEEP
FRANCES: OK. Thanks for your help. Bye.

Track 9.3

a Can I speak to Lila?
b Are you busy?
c Do you want me to call later?
d When can I have it back?
e What can I do for you?
f How are you?

Track 9.4

LILA: Hello?
BEEP
LILA: Speaking.
BEEP
LILA: Fine, thanks.
BEEP
LILA: Yes, actually. I am a little.
BEEP
LILA: No, that's OK. What can I do for you?
BEEP
LILA: Oh, right. Well, I have bad news for you.

Track 9.5

a can't
b couldn't
c could
d message
e managed
f busy

Track 10.1

1
YOUNG MAN: It's just what I wanted.
GRANDMA: I'm glad you like it.
2
YOUNG MAN: Thank you for all your help.
YOUNG WOMAN: You're welcome.
3
WOMAN: Thanks to you the party was a great success.
OLD WOMAN: It was a pleasure.
4
YOUNG WOMAN: Thanks so much for helping me with my homework.
OLDER MAN: No problem.
5
WOMAN: Thanks a lot for dinner.
MAN: Don't mention it.

Track 10.2

a
BEEP
YOUR FRIEND: You're welcome.
b
YOUR FRIEND: Thanks so much for the great DVD. I love it.
BEEP
c
BEEP
YOUR BROTHER: No problem.
d
BEEP
YOUR MOTHER: I'm so glad you liked it.

Track 10.3

a thank
b with
c that
d three
e north
f mother
g thirty
h mouth
i father
j this

Track 10.4

a Don't forget to thank your mother.
b Do you think he's thirty?
c This is my father.

d Don't put that in your mouth.

e There's the person who's from the north.

Track 10.5

a thank

b think

c send

d owe

e cash

f receipt

g unwrap

Track 11.1

a

MIKE: Have you ever eaten octopus?

LAURA: Yes, I tried it last year.

MIKE: Did you like it?

LAURA: Yes, it was delicious.

b

CINDY: I saw a great movie last night. It's called 'Escape from the Edge'. Have you seen it?

BRAD: No, I haven't been to the cinema for a long time, but I went to the theatre last week.

CINDY: Really? What did you see?

BRAD: It was a play called 'A Merry Life'.

Track 11.2

a It was awful. So boring. It was slow and really romantic and I didn't find it enjoyable at all.

b Wow! What a great movie – it had lots of action and I found it so enjoyable. It was really good fun watching the cars racing through the streets of a large city.

c It was so scary! I had to close my eyes most of the time. There were these people killing other people – it was so violent.

d I loved it! It was so funny – I laughed from beginning to end. These movies are so enjoyable. I wish there were more movies like this one.

Track 11.3

a Have you seen 'Days of Laughter'?

BEEP

b Have you seen 'Night of the Zombie Killers'?

BEEP

c Have you seen 'The Long Hot Summer'?

BEEP

d Have you seen 'The New York Race'?

BEEP

Track 11.4

MAN: Murray's Restaurant here.

WOMAN: Hello. I'd like to book a table, please.

MAN: Certainly. What day is that for?

WOMAN: Next Wednesday, please.

MAN: Sure. And how many people is that for?

WOMAN: Just for two.

MAN: Two people on Wednesday. OK, and what time were you thinking of?

WOMAN: 8 o'clock.

MAN: 8pm. Right. And what's your name?

WOMAN: Jennifer Healey.

MAN: OK, Ms Healey. Next Wednesday at 8 o'clock, table for two.

WOMAN: Thank you very much.

RECEPTIONIST: The Garden Hotel. Can I help you?

MAN: Yes, I'd like a room for two nights, please.

RECEPTIONIST: Two nights? Is that for tonight?

MAN: Yes, tonight and tomorrow night.

RECEPTIONIST: I'm afraid the hotel is full tonight.

MAN: Oh dear. What about tomorrow?

RECEPTIONIST: We have one room available tomorrow.

MAN: OK, can I book that room, please?

RECEPTIONIST: Certainly sir. Can I have your credit card number?

MAN: Yes. It's 6475 7564 …. [fade]

Track 11.5

MAN: Murray's Restaurant here.

BEEP

MAN: Certainly. What day is that for?

BEEP

MAN: Sure. And how many people is that for?

BEEP

MAN: OK, and what time were you thinking of?

BEEP

MAN: Right. And what's your name?

BEEP

MAN: OK. Your table is booked.

BEEP

RECEPTIONIST: The Garden Hotel. Can I help you?

BEEP

RECEPTIONIST: Is that for tonight?

BEEP

RECEPTIONIST: I'm afraid the hotel is full tonight.

BEEP

RECEPTIONIST: We have one room available tomorrow.

BEEP

RECEPTIONIST: Certainly sir. Can I have your credit card number.

BEEP

Track 11.6

a We went to see my mother yesterday.

b I don't feel like going to the party.

c What a terrible movie.

d She's coming to see you?

e Take this away immediately.

f Oh no! That's very bad news.

g I think she's going home soon.

Track 11.7

a never
b audience
c rehearse
d relax
e clap
f performance
g since
h scary
i violent
j credit card

Track 12.1

Conversation a

WOMAN: Would you like me to help you with dinner?
MAN: Thanks. That would be great. Can you chop those onions?

Conversation b

YOUNG MAN: You look tired. How about if I make you a nice cup of tea?
OLD LADY: Thanks, dear, but I'm fine. I'll have some tea later.

Conversation c

OLD MAN: I can't open this door.
YOUNG MAN: Allow me. It is very heavy.

Conversation d

YOUNG WOMAN: Why don't you do the first part of the reading and I'll do the second part, so we save time.
YOUNG MAN: Sure. It's about 100 pages altogether.

Conversation e

YOUNG WOMAN: Can I help you to do the shopping?
OLD WOMAN: Don't worry about it. I only need to get a few things.

Track 12.2

a DAD: Would you like me to help you, son?
BEEP
DAD: Oh, OK.
b YOUNG MAN: Wow! What a mess! How about if we help you to get the room ready?
BEEP
YOUNG MAN: Right. OK.

Track 12.3

Pair A

1 You have to say 'good boy'.
2 You have to say 'good bye'.

Pair B

1 Can I look at that tie?
2 Can I look at that toy?

Pair C

1 Be careful! Don't slip on the oil!
2 Be careful! Don't slip in the aisle.

Pair D

1 Would you like to, Troy?
2 Would you like to try?

Track 12.4

a speech
b planted
c won't
d thanks
e clown
f clone
g may
h might

Track 13.1

KRISTINA: Ellie, what does talent mean?
ELLIE: Oh, it means something that you are good at.
KRISTINA: OK, I understand. Like I have a talent for singing.
ELLIE: That's right.
KRISTINA: And what do you call it when you like doing something, even if you are not good at it?
ELLIE: You mean, like a hobby?
KRISTINA: Yes, a hobby.
ELLIE: Usually people who have hobbies have some kind of ability for the thing they like to do, but not always.
KRISTINA: What do you mean by ability?
ELLIE: Ability means being able to do something, like an activity.
KRISTINA: Activity? What's that?
ELLIE: An activity is something you do.
KRISTINA: Wow! I need a dictionary. Then I could find these words for myself. How do you say find out something for yourself?
ELLIE: Discover. Yes, I think you need a dictionary, Kristina.

Track 13.2

ABBY: I really don't like parties.
BEEP
CHRIS: Shy? Are you shy?
BEEP
CHRIS: You mean, it frightens you.
BEEP
CHRIS: That's strange, because you're very popular.
BEEP
CHRIS: It's when a lot of people like you.
BEEP
CHRIS: Oh, you mean when people pay you a lot of attention.
BEEP

Track 13.3

a We're gonna go to the beach.
b She's going to win.
c James is going to study French.
d They're gonna tell you to stop.

Track 13.4

a She's going to win.
b I'm going to go to Paris.
c Are you going to go to the party?
d Is he going to play?

Track 14.1

JAYNE: What's the most delicious meal you've ever eaten?

DAVID: I'll have to think.

JAYNE: Take your time.

DAVID: It was the meal my mum cooked for my eighteenth birthday.

JAYNE: What did she cook?

DAVID: She made roast chicken with roast potatoes and gravy.

JAYNE: That sounds nice.

DAVID: Yes, everyone loved it!

Track 14.2

MAN: What was the most delicious meal you've ever eaten?

BEEP

MAN: Who cooked it?

BEEP

MAN: What did that person (or people) cook?

BEEP

Track 14.3

beautiful
ugly
delicious
horrible
enjoyable
boring
frightening
bad
cheap
cramped
deep
expensive
fast
fat
funny
good
high
interesting
long
narrow
spacious
thin
uncomfortable

Track 14.4

a beautiful
b delicious
c boring
d enjoyable
e frightening
f funny
g expensive
h interesting
i spacious
j narrow
k uncomfortable

Track 14.5

a dramatic
b modern
c ugly
d diva
e minute
f enormous
g shallow
h wide
i worst
j shortest

Track 15.1

RICHARD: I need to wear glasses.

ALICE: So do I. I can't read the newspaper very well.

RICHARD: Neither can I. It gives me a headache.

ALICE: Me too! But I don't know any good opticians.

RICHARD: Neither do I, but my sister knows one.

ALICE: That's good. Can you give me the name when you've asked her?

RICHARD: Sure. I need to have my eyes tested soon.

ALICE: I do, too. Call me tonight, I'm not going out.

RICHARD: I'm not either. I'll call you around seven.

ALICE: OK. Thanks.

Track 15.2

MARIA: Hi, my name's Maria Smith.

BEEP

MARIA: Oh really? Where are you from?

BEEP

MARIA: Me too! Where do you live?

BEEP

MARIA: So do I. Are you married?

BEEP

MARIA: Neither am I. What do you do?

BEEP

MARIA: I'm a student, too. What are you studying?

BEEP

MARIA: No, I'm not. I'm studying psychology.

Track 15.3

a

MAN: He put the car in the garage.

WOMAN: He put the car in the garage.

b

MAN: The paint is in the garage.

WOMAN: The paint is in the garage.

c

MAN: John is upstairs in his room.

WOMAN: John is upstairs in his room.

d

MAN: What do you think of this room?

WOMAN: What do you think of this room?

e

MAN: I really need some new shoes.

WOMAN: I really need some new shoes.

f

MAN: This DVD is new.
WOMAN: This DVD is new.

Track 15.4

a either
either

b neither
neither

c room
room

d garage
garage

e new
new

Track 16.1

JANE: So, let me tell you about what happened at the airport.
ROBBIE: Uh-huh.
JANE: Well, I arrived early to check in.
ROBBIE: Right.
JANE: And then I went to get something to eat.
ROBBIE: Uh-huh.
JANE: While I was eating a sandwich I heard someone scream.
ROBBIE: Then what happened?
JANE: Well, I ran to where I heard the scream.
ROBBIE: Yeah?
JANE: And, you'll never guess what?
ROBBIE: What?
JANE: There was nobody there.
ROBBIE: That's weird. What happened next?
JANE: Well, I looked and looked everywhere for the person in trouble.
ROBBIE: And?
JANE: I never found anything. And do you know what was the worst thing?
ROBBIE: What?
JANE: I missed the plane, because I was looking for the person who screamed.
ROBBIE: Wow!

Track 16.2

JANE: So, let me tell you about what happened at the airport.
BEEP
JANE: Well, I arrived early to check in.
BEEP
JANE: And then I went to get something to eat.
BEEP
JANE: While I was eating a sandwich I heard someone scream.
BEEP
JANE: Well, I ran to where I heard the scream.
BEEP
JANE: And, you'll never guess what?
BEEP

JANE: There was nobody there.
BEEP
JANE: Well, I looked and looked everywhere for the person in trouble.
BEEP
JANE: I never found anything. And do you know what was the worst thing?
BEEP
JANE: I missed the plane, because I was looking for the person who screamed.
BEEP

Track 16.3

a U-N-I-D-E-N-T-I-F-I-E-D new word F-L-Y-I-N-G new word O-B-J-E-C-T

b D-I-G-I-T-A-L new word V-I-D-E-O new word D-I-S-C

c B-R-I-T-I-S-H new word B-R-O-A-D-C-A-S-T-I-N-G new word C-O-R-P-O-R-A-T-I-O-N

d U-N-I-T-E-D new word S-T-A-T-E-S new word O-F new word A-M-E-R-I-C-A

Track 16.4

MAN: Two women were walking through a local cemetery filming with a video camera. Suddenly the camera stopped working. They kept taping with a portable tape recorder that one woman had in her pocket. They chatted about the beauty of the cemetery as they walked along the path. Later when they listened to the recording, they heard something very strange. After one of the women said 'What a peaceful area,' a creepy whisper said 'peaceful.' They played the tape about 20 times and heard the voice each time.

Track 16.5

a weird

b scary

c amazing

d spectators

e sunblock

f wow

g UFO

h BBC

Table of phonemic symbols

Consonants

Symbol	Example
p	please
b	better
t	truth
d	dark
k	class
g	go
f	finish
v	very
θ	thin
ð	that
s	sing
z	zoo
ʃ	shop
ʒ	measure
h	help
x	loch
tʃ	children
dʒ	join
m	some
n	son
ŋ	sing
w	wait
l	late
r	read
j	yes

Vowels

	Symbol	Example
short	ɪ	sit
	e	said
	æ	bat
	ɒ	top
	ʌ	luck
	ʊ	foot
	ə	again
long	iː	sleep
	ɑː	car
	ɔː	forward
	uː	school
	ɜː	heard
diphthongs	eɪ	lake
	aɪ	tie
	ɔɪ	joy
	əʊ	go
	aʊ	wow!
	ɪə	peculiar
	eə	air
	ʊə	cruel

Track list

CD Track no.	Unit	Activity Track no.	Activity and Page	CD Track no.	Unit	Activity Track no.	Activity and Page
1	1	1.1	Act. 4, Page 6	41	9	9.1	Act. 10 & 11, Page 48
2	1	1.2	Act. 5, Page 6	42	9	9.2	Act. 12, Page 49
3	1	1.3	Act. 13, Page 8	43	9	9.3	Act. 13 & 14, Page 49
4	1	1.4	Act. 17, Page 9	44	9	9.4	Act. 15, Page 49
5	2	2.1	Act. 9, Page 13	45	9	9.5	Act. 18, Page 50
6	2	2.2	Act. 10, Page 13	46	10	10.1	Act. 7, Page 53
7	2	2.3	Act. 11, Page 13	47	10	10.2	Act. 9, Page 53
8	2	2.4	Act. 12, Page 13	48	10	10.3	Act. 10, Page 54
9	2	2.5	Act. 15, Page 14	49	10	10.4	Act. 11, Page 54
10	3	3.1	Act. 11, Page 18	50	10	10.5	Act. 16, Page 55
11	3	3.2	Act. 12, Page 18	51	11	11.1	Act. 2, Page 56
12	3	3.3	Act. 14, Page 18	52	11	11.2	Act. 4, Page 57
13	3	3.4	Act. 15 Page 18	53	11	11.3	Act. 5, Page 57
14	3	3.5	Act. 18, Page 19	54	11	11.4	Act. 9, Page 59
15	4	4.1	Act. 7, Page 21	55	11	11.5	Act. 10, Page 59
16	4	4.2	Act. 8, Page 21	56	11	11.6	Act. 11, Page 59
17	4	4.3	Act. 12, Page 23	57	11	11.7	Act. 15, Page 60
18	4	4.4	Act. 14, Page 23	58	12	12.1	Act. 7, Page 63
19	4	4.5	Act. 17, Page 24	59	12	12.2	Act. 8, Page 63
20	5	5.1	Act. 8, Page 27	60	12	12.3	Act. 9, Page 64
21	5	5.2	Act. 9, Page 27	61	12	12.4	Act. 15, Page 65
22	5	5.3	Act. 10, Page 27	62	13	13.1	Act. 1, Page 66
23	5	5.4	Act. 16, Page 29	63	13	13.2	Act. 3, Page 66
24	6	6.1	Act. 4, Page 31	64	13	13.3	Act. 7, Page 68
25	6	6.2	Act. 6, Page 31	65	13	13.4	Act. 16, Page 70
26	6	6.3	Act. 7, Page 31	66	14	14.1	Act. 12, Page 73
27	6	6.4	Act. 11, Page 33	67	14	14.2	Act. 13, Page 73
28	6	6.5	Act. 12, Page 33	68	14	14.3	Act. 14, Page 74
29	6	6.6	Act. 13, Page 33	69	14	14.4	Act. 15, Page 74
30	6	6.7	Act. 16, Page 34	70	14	14.5	Act. 18, Page 75
31	7	7.1	Act. 7, Page 37	71	15	15.1	Act. 7, Page 78
32	7	7.2	Act. 9, Page 37	72	15	15.2	Act. 9, Page 78
33	7	7.3	Act. 10 & 11, Page 37	73	15	15.3	Act. 10 & 11, Page 79
34	7	7.4	Act. 12, Page 37	74	15	15.4	Act. 17, Page 80
35	7	7.5	Act. 18, Page 39	75	16	16.1	Act. 9, Page 83
36	8	8.1	Act. 9, Page 42	76	16	16.2	Act. 10, Page 83
37	8	8.2	Act. 10, Page 42	77	16	16.3	Act. 11, Page 83
38	8	8.3	Act.15, Page 44	78	16	16.4	Act. 12, Page 84
39	8	8.4	Act. 16, Page 44	79	16	16.5	Act.15, Page 85
40	8	8.5	Act. 19, Page 45				